...me + Brian,

God blessed me big ...th my trip to CCI - Not ...ly with Excel but my entire ...i family.

May you continue to shine your lights this world and make it a better place!

With Love + Blessings

Karen

D1369836

BETWEEN TWO WORLDS

Bridging the Gap
From Silence to Sound

Karen S. Londos

ParkerHouseBooks.com
2013 Edition 1

ISBN: 978-0-9895474-1-3

What people are saying...

"*Between Two Worlds is an insightful experience, as Karen exhibits courage and clarity in sharing her personal story with the world. It reinforced my own awareness and sensitivity to resist assumptions and really take the time to get to know others because appearances are often deceiving. We often look upon the appearance of lack or struggle as obstacles to stop us when all the time there is a bigger plan and design at play. Karen's journey enlightened me and I shall now remember to walk in faith instead of fear and I shall not judge or presume to know another's journey. My purpose is to share love and compassion and this book did a great job evoking those emotions from me.*"

~Nancy Matthews
Founder of Women's Prosperity Network and best-selling author of Visionaries with Guts *and* The One Philosophy

"*Karen has created a masterpiece that is rich in content, rich in reality, and rich in spirit. This book will be the saving grace and the connection many people in today's time need. This book is a thorough exploration of what it really takes to get over your challenges and embrace your strengths. It will push you to show up in the world differently and I highly recommend it!*

~Lucinda Cross

Best Selling Author of The Road to Redemption

Acknowledgements

First and foremost I thank God for his unending love and guidance, knowing that without it I would be a lost soul. I am grateful for every experience and the assurance that He is preparing the path before me, wherever it may lead.

There are so many people to thank as we travel through this journey we call life: So many that become a part of our lives and contribute to who we become. I treasure every person that has crossed my path, knowing there was a divine purpose served by their presence, however brief.

To my wonderful children, Chad and Devin. You have made every minute of my life worth living and I am so proud of the wonderful people you have become. Choose to be happy, cherish your life and be all that you were destined to be: Believe!

To my sisters, Sheryl, Lori and Nanci, and their families. Forever Family. Forever Friends. Forever Loved. I could not have made it through this past year without you. Thank you for gently loving me through learning to be vulnerable.

To Kimmy and Christy, cousins by blood but sisters at heart. When it is all said and done, there is nothing more important than family. Thank you for always being there.

To my beautiful daughter-in-law, Heather. I thank God every day for all that you have brought to our family and for the wonderful wife and Mother you are.

I rest easy knowing my son has met his soulmate and my grandchildren have the best of the best in a Mother.

To my precious Angel, Camryn. You will always be my Schnookem-books. I love you more than chocolate chip cookies and ice cream!

To Chris, my friend, my mentor and my encourager. You have been an Angel since God placed you next to me at the Unconference where you went above and beyond for a stranger. You are a true inspiration! Thank you for your continued support and encouragement.

A special thanks to Dr. Yvonne Oswald, for not only your wonderful editing but your guidance and positive energy over the course of the last year. You are a genuine soul and a rare breed.

This book is dedicated
To M.K.
A reason, A season. But in my heart
A lifetime. Thanks for leading me back to me.

Introduction

My story is different. So many books begin with a tale of overcoming childhood adversity. Through strength, perseverance and nothing less than the grace of God the person scratches and claws their way forward to become a huge success story and inspire people the world over. I don't have such a story to share. What I do have is a story that probably fits millions and can touch millions; it is, in its own way, extraordinary. The fact is that we are all extraordinary and we all have a story to tell that can impact someone; sometimes many more someones than we even realize. Some stories are worth the telling.

Table of Contents

Chapter I

Navigating the Hearing World

I was ten years old. The teacher asked a question and I shot my hand up thinking I had the answer. When she called on me I stood up and proudly gave the answer I thought she was looking for, and the entire class laughed out loud. The laughter probably lasted less than a minute but for me, at that moment, it felt like an eternity. What had I said? Something was not right. I laughed with them, disguising my deeper retreat into a world of silence and fear with an outward show of bravado and confidence. I didn't know it then, but this was the start of a journey that would take me in search of answers to a question I didn't even know to ask. This was the beginning of the end for the brave girl eager to shine; my confidence got replaced by shyness and the desire to just blend in. It was not until years later, when my deafness became more profound I realized that, even in those early years as I plunged deeper into retreat, I was facing and beginning to overcome a challenge that I did not yet know existed.

If You Could Hear What I Don't

I was born with a degenerative hearing loss; nerve endings that never fully developed prohibiting me from hearing high pitched frequencies from birth and then gradually the remainder of the hearing lessening with time. High frequency hearing loss affects your ability to understand speech. Consonant letters are considered high frequency and therefore most sound the same, making understanding what people are saying not easy. I would complain of the noise or loudness yet not understand what was going on because I could not distinguish the sounds; they were just sounds. So I was the first to say, "The TV is too loud.", "Why are you shouting?" or "What is that noise?" leading people to make comments that I had selective hearing. I always had the urge to say "I wish!" I'm sure I probably did say it more than once.

Have you ever had someone say to you, "I wish I could be inside of your head to know what you're thinking?" Well there are many times I wish, as I'm sure many deaf people do, that there was a way for the hearing world to grasp what our world is like. One of the biggest issues that surfaced over and over again in my research of those that are partially deaf was that people don't realize the extent of the challenge because we are articulate and communicate with ease, or so it appears. Getting through a day is not easy. I use extreme concentration not only in listening but in speaking. I read lips. I read body language. The brain is very powerful but it is still working overtime to make the adjustments needed for me to function on a daily basis. The doctor once told me I hear less than even I know because the brain is so powerful it adapts as needed. As described to me, my common sense takes over in many cases. My brain has a data base of words, so that when someone says something that I hear incorrectly, my brain knows it doesn't make sense and it immediately refers to my data base and finds the word that fits. For example I might hear "Would you like some KEY?" but my brain realizes that doesn't make sense so it searches the data base and comes back with TEA. All of this takes place within seconds so that I don't even know I didn't hear correctly.

As I mentioned earlier, when people are articulate and seem to communicate with ease the challenge is brushed over. As an example, several years ago I was at the doctor's having a series of tests done because my migraines were getting progressively worse. When I filled out the paperwork for the doctor I wrote that I had a hearing loss and was a lip reader. He ordered a test that hooked up electrodes to my head, and then a headset was put on. The headset made all kinds of noises and it tested how quickly the brainwaves reacted to the noises. I had to do nothing but simply lie there for 30 minutes. When they explained the test to me I made the joke, "Hope the brain waves respond quicker than my ears do." Well, apparently not. After the test, I asked the tech, "So, did it tell you anything?" She replied, "The test was inclusive because you don't hear well do you?" You think! When I went back to the doctor he showed me the remarks of the tech, which read "This test was inconclusive because this patient is profoundly deaf." He looked at me very apologetically and said, "I'm so sorry. I know you told me you don't hear well but I really didn't grasp the depth of it. You communicate so well and are so articulate, one would never know." I wasn't sure if I should be flattered or bill him for my out of pocket expenses.

Hearing aids are a major adjustment; it's like wearing microphones on your ears. Then there is the new technology of cochlear implants (CIs). I recently watched a YouTube video that gave a great explanation of how a person with CIs hears as compared to a hearing person. CIs give off a very mechanical sound; I recall my father saying everyone sounded like Robbie Robot. In essence, whatever type of assistive device that is being used, it is an attempt to make a deaf person into a hearing person and that is not possible. Oh it's possible to make them hear things, but not in the same way as a hearing person. For some, the adjustment to assistive devices is not worth the outcome and that has to be respected. They are not for everyone. I first began wearing aids at the age of 22 years and wore them until my mid 30's. At that point one broke and because my hearing had taken another major decline I needed new ones anyway. Unfortunately, most insurance does not cover the cost of hearing aids and at the time I was not in a financial situation to purchase them so I did without. Modern medicine has come a long way but still it's an adjustment to utilize assistive devices. I adjusted rather quickly when I first began wearing them with the only real adjustment being the background noise. In certain situations the background noise would become so loud that I would have to take the aids out. And while there were certain noises that I never heard, or had not heard for a period of time, I still had enough hearing to adapt to the new noises that were introduced.

I remember vividly some of the sounds that I had never heard, or perhaps had heard at a very young age but didn't remember. Like the noise a zipper makes. I remember when my father first got his aids we tiptoed around the house for weeks so as not to scare the living daylights out of him with noises. He told the story of getting dressed for work one morning and when he pulled the zipper up on his pants he about jumped out of his skin. So I was very anxious to hear this noise when I got my hearing aids. Well I'll be darned, my dad was right, that sucker makes a loud noise when you pull it up and down. I remember sitting in my car laughing, just doing things to make noise to see what it sounded like. It's really not easy to explain that feeling of hearing things that you never knew made noise. I didn't realize what I was missing. You know the famous saying, "You never miss it until it's gone." Well for people like me who learn from birth and/or gradually to compensate over the course of time, most times we aren't even aware anything is missing. But for me, I used to wonder. I would sit outside at night and ask, "What do you hear?" for all I heard was silence for the most part. Even with aids I was unable to hear many sounds. I wanted to know what a bird sounded like. How about a frog? What exactly does *tweet* or *ribbit* sound like? I still don't really know but I did discover, with my second 'attempt' at hearing aids after going without for many years, what a cricket, or as those of us from the north call them, what a 'Katydid' sounds like. THE MOST ANNOYING sound I could imagine! True story: I was just fitted with new hearing aids after almost 10 years of going without and as I left the doctor's office everything came crashing in. I could hear many things but had no idea what the sounds were or where they were coming from - the wind, the trees, shoes clacking on the ground and the ever wonder of a KATIEDID. Visiting my cousin and trying to enjoy a family dinner, as my mother and sister were in town, we sat on the back porch of my cousin's home to enjoy the very rare cool South Florida evening. There was this horrid noise. The best I can describe it is the sound of trying to say the letter T, but thousands and thousands of them all at once, and so loud! As I looked around the patio at the others, they were perfectly content, engaged in conversation and not at all bothered by this thousand times T sound. After several minutes, and a moment of thinking I might lose my mind if it didn't stop I finally said "Does anyone else here that noise?" "What noise" was the response so I mimicked the noise the best I could and my mother, laughed and very calmly said "Oh, that, those are katydids." To which my reply was "Can someone please tell Katie to don't because it's driving me insane!" Needless to say the hearing aids came out at that point for a break.

Noises the hearing world take for granted are like amplified sounds coming from everywhere and for me, I cannot determine what the sound is or the direction it is coming from. Much of the challenge to adjust stemmed from living in years of silence and the doctors did warn that it would take me some time to get used to hearing some of the noises. The final straw was when I chased around a noise in my office one night for a good ten minutes, trying to figure out what it was and where it was coming from.

When I finally realized that every time I heard the sound I got that feeling in my stomach when you get hungry, I realized the term "My stomach is growling." really meant it made noise! Who knew? In addition to all the unidentifiable noises there was no advantage at all trying to talk on the phone, which was the main reason I wanted them. I could not hear on the phone at all with them and would take them out each time I had to make or receive a call. So I retreated back to my silent world which I had become quite accustomed to, but not without the judgment of those around me. They said I gave up; that I wasn't trying. In my mind it was like saying that I fell short yet again. But there are so many factors involved and the reality is that, even with the greatest technology around, you cannot make a deaf person hear as a normal person does; it's not the same. So it's not hiding or quitting, or giving up. It is accepting my reality as it is and dealing with it in the best way for me.

I have many advantages due to my uniqueness. I don't hear but I listen more intently than most hearing individuals. If you're talking to me you can be sure you DO have my full attention. You can talk to me while I run the vacuum at the same time; makes no difference to me either way. It is all about perception and when we train ourselves to perceive positively, then you see the advantages of your situation and you embrace those. As crazy as it was, while I hid behind so many masks I was still able to see the glass half full. I have entertained the idea of trying again with hearing aids or even a Cochlear Implant but whether that happens or not doesn't matter. I have adjusted to my uniqueness and continue to move forward, allowing nothing to stand in my way.

Breaking through the Barrier

My paternal grandmother was, for all practical purposes, deaf. She couldn't talk on the phone. She couldn't hear you with her back to you. My grandfather used to stomp on the floor so the vibration would get her attention. I remember she really didn't like that! She also couldn't stand it when people would shout at her. I can relate. It drives me crazy! Shouting doesn't help. Sitting in front of her you would never know there was an issue. She was an expert lip reader and she spoke fine, aside from her slight Polish accent. I loved my grandmother and I was in awe of her as a young girl; she functioned so well with such a challenge and it amazed me. Little did I know I would one day be wearing her shoes. This was a genetic issue that affected all of her siblings and both of her children. My father however did not embrace his challenge in the beginning; he chose to pretend it didn't exist for many years. I guess he wore his masks too. The apple doesn't fall far from the tree.

Research estimates that 50 million Americans suffer from some degree of hearing loss and for many the cause is unknown. Determining the cause of hearing loss is complicated due to the many factors that may be involved, both genetically as well as environmentally. Although diagnosed in my early teens, it was after the birth of my son, in my early twenties, that I experienced a dramatic decline in my hearing and began wearing aids. While I didn't know it at the time, I was told after the birth of my second child and had another major decline that there was a direct correlation between the pregnancies and the decline in my hearing. The doctor told me if I had any more kids I would probably go totally deaf. They said they didn't know exactly what the connection was but it had been proven that pregnancy directly affected the hearing for 'people with my issue'. I have never to this day gotten a straight answer or 'diagnosis' as to what my issue exactly is. Does it have a name? They just say degenerative hearing loss due to nerve endings that never developed.

Because deafness is an invisible condition and it varies in degree, it is sometimes not easy to grasp the extent of the loss. For those us with partial deafness, degenerative losses and/or those that have utilized assistive devices and speech therapy from a young age, we have learned to articulate well and read lips with ease so when we say we are deaf/hard of hearing there is a measure of disbelief from others. Many of us have learned to navigate the hearing world with relative ease, despite the daily challenge and the lack of understanding from the hearing world. There is a huge difference in being deaf (lowercase, medical term) and Deaf (uppercase, a culture) and with that difference is a lack of understanding and sometimes misplaced compassion which often leaves the deaf individual feeling like a misfit. There is a sense of being stuck so to speak between two worlds because we are not Deaf (uppercase), nor are we fully hearing. When one refers to a person who is deaf, it is a medical term for a degree of hearing loss which covers a wide range, from profound to slight. Research shows that the perception of deafness as a disability promotes emotional stigmas and lower self esteem in some and socially it promotes discrimination. For years the majority looked at deafness as a disability and there was a stigma attached to those that were deaf as not being as intelligent. This mentality still exists today, which is why the Deaf Culture was established.

"Rewriting deaf to Deaf is about disowning an imposed medicalized identity and developing an empowered identity rooted in a community and culture of others who share similar experiences and outlooks on the world." [1] It is about shedding the stigma of being disabled and developing an empowerment of simply having a different way of life. So if you are part of the Deaf Culture, you have adopted a lifestyle unlike those that are deaf or hearing, much like if you are Amish or a member of a First Nations Tribe. It is an accepted way of living in a tight knit community where outsiders are not often easily accepted. For me, this is understandable, as I know the trials in navigating the hearing world and experience similar prejudices as those of the Deaf Culture. Look at the simple fact that even audiologist or ENT offices don't regularly have a signer on staff. While I'm not fluent in sign, wouldn't it make sense to have a fluent speaker of the language used in the places where the Deaf go to get hearing checks? I live in South Florida where there is a large population of Latin descent and to get a job in this area often requires knowing how to speak Spanish. This is to accommodate the vast number of foreigners that speak only Spanish in this area. Why would we not make the same concession for our own Deaf citizens who speak another language that is not always of their choosing?

So on one hand you have the Deaf Culture that uses another language (American Sign Language) that is not easily accepting of outsiders and on the other hand you have the hearing world that doesn't

---

[1] Bauman 2008, Page 9

understand a condition which lies beneath the surface and is not visible to the naked eye. In researching for this book, one of the common denominators amongst the partially deaf is the shared frustration level of feeling like they are on the outside of both worlds. We don't sign so it's almost impossible to live within the Deaf Culture. It's like going to a foreign country where you don't speak the language. Even if you sign, you are often not accepted into the Deaf community because they feel like you are going against their empowerment beliefs.

The hearing world is only slightly easier to navigate but still lacks the understanding of what it takes for a deaf individual to get through the day. As lip readers, we clearly need strategic positioning with the person or people we are talking or listening to. To hold these conversations takes a huge amount of concentration, not only to follow the conversation, but to speak as well. For many of us masters of articulation it is not something that flows easily. This also takes an enormous amount of concentration to make sure we are pronouncing correctly and clearly. It's exhausting at times to get through a day and by the end of it we have family members telling us we're mumbling, we're slurring or we're talking like we have a hair (cleft) lip. Which is rather comical; since we are deaf we have no idea what that even means except to surmise that it impedes the speech. Myself, I began to seclude myself and not participate in events where there were large groups. If I did find myself in the situation, whether personally or professionally, I scoped out the nearest non-conspicuous location, usually a corner, and parked myself there for the duration. I became quite the expert at blending in; at being invisible. Ironically this was the very thing I had fought so much against. As a lip reader, you can only read one set of lips at a time and you must be strategically placed to be able to do this if you are not talking one on one. It was too frustrating, not to mention demeaning at the thought of looking unintelligent if questions were asked and I had no idea what was going on. Due to the stigma that deaf equates to a lower capacity to learn people make assumptions that deaf individuals lack intelligence to some degree. It's also difficult as a lip reader to communicate with most individuals that speak English as a second language. They pronounce their words differently which makes it not easy for us to understand. For me it just became easier to avoid the situation altogether. So in large groups in particular I became like a recluse. People would say I was so shy and those that knew me well were like "HUH?" However when I was put in a large crowd even with people I knew I often became very quiet, resulting in everyone asking me if I was ok or upset about something. My true personality is outgoing and bubbly. I have a great sarcastic sense of humor (at least I think I'm pretty funny) and love to make people laugh and feel good. But that was lost somewhere along the way in any environment outside my closest circle, which was small considering I didn't allow many to infiltrate that circle.

I can relate to the Deaf Culture and their closed society, because on my own level I had done the same. The difference was I didn't benefit from the camaraderie that the Deaf Culture enjoys. I will never forget the instantaneous bonds that formed when I spent two weeks training with my Hearing Dog. There were nine of us with different degrees of deafness but the commonality of some hearing with assistive devices and the use of lip reading as our main source of communication. We immediately developed our own culture so to speak because we understood each other and the challenges we faced. It was like we had known each other forever. Each night after training we sat around 'the big table' until late into the night talking and laughing and sharing our experiences. We could finish each other's sentences because we had been there and knew the conclusion. I don't think I ever laughed so much before or since those two weeks and it was an emotional breakthrough. I not only left Santa Rosa with my Hearing Dog I left with eight new friends and the realization that I was not alone; there really are others similar to me that understand my journey through this life.

After my return home I was eating breakfast at a local restaurant and I met a woman who had been deaf since the age of three. Denise was a lovely lady who was intrigued with my service dog and so she struck up a conversation. She asked about my dog and my hearing loss and what I did for a living. We stood in the middle of the restaurant talking for several minutes, after which time her husband joined us. He commented something to the effect that in all the years they had been together he had never known her to talk to anyone for that long. She made a comment that was an 'AHA' moment for me, and it sent me on the journey of writing this book. She said "We (she and her husband) live half in the deaf world and half in the hearing world because...." And as she trailed off I finished the sentence "Because we don't quite fit in either world." Her eyes welled up and she said "Yes, you understand." I did. It was the first time I actually verbalized it and it was a profound moment for me because I had never quite put my finger on it until that moment. A total stranger put my finger on it. We were stuck between two worlds. Again, it was an instantaneous bond. We exchanged numbers and met again several weeks later for the first time to get to know each other. We met at 8:30 in the morning for breakfast and we were still there at 12:30pm. It was as if we had known each other our entire lives. Denise's story is included in the final Chapter of this book, along with other unique and inspiring individuals that have overcome and been inspired by their own challenges.

The Angel with a Tail

I never really had a fear of not hearing and I guess I never dwelled on it much either. I simply learned to make concessions along the way as the need arose; some consciously and others unconsciously. At one point several years back I did some research on Hearing dogs but wasn't sure of the benefit for me. If I can't teach the dog to answer the phone and translate for me what could I use him for? And it was still a dog after all. It needed walked and fed and taken care of. And the hair.......ahhh, no. I just didn't think it was for me. That was only until one situation made me realize I could be in danger at times and not even know it.

It was early evening and I was working at a client's office alone. I was in one of the offices near the front but the front door was not visible from where I sat. Suddenly, there was a continuous, hard pounding on the front door, loud enough to startle even me. It was after dark and a bit leery, I cautiously rounded the corner to see who was making the racket. Standing at the door were three very handsome firemen, two banging feverishly to get my attention and all looking at me in annoyance, like I had no sense whatsoever. Aside from the fact they had been knocking for several minutes, it seemed the fire alarm was ringing and due to the lack of functioning strobes I was oblivious to any danger. Fortunately it was a false alarm but it could have been a very serious situation for me. It was this incident that provoked me into accepting the reality that a challenge did exist that could be a potential danger so I began to investigate the possibility of a service dog, more seriously this time.

I located Canine Companions for Independence (CCI) in Orlando, Florida, a non-profit organization only three hours away and what I liked most was they breed their own dogs, using Golden and Labrador Retrievers. I gathered all the needed information, filled out the application and then sat on it for almost a year. I kept going back and forth. It would be safer for me. I wouldn't miss so many phone calls. But it could affect my career. What if people weren't receptive ? Back and forth: Should I or shouldn't I? Ironically, my sister lived in Orlando and she started a new job. Her immediate supervisor was a volunteer puppy raiser for CCI. She called to tell me and ask me if I had ever turned in my application. No. So she spoke to someone at the center and we were invited to an upcoming graduation where two board members, both with Hearing Dogs, would be attending. My sister and I attended the graduation and I was fortunate to speak to these two wonderful people that answered all my questions and my doubts about the service dog.

I returned home and immediately turned in my paperwork. The first part of the process, from the time I turned in my application, did an initial online chat interview, a follow up interview at CCI in Orlando and then received my letter of acceptance took approximately four months. Then I was placed on the wait list, which was an estimated eighteen to twenty four months. The Hearing Dogs were only trained on the main campus in Santa Rosa, CA and they usually had four to six applicants in training at a time. So the wait began. It was a long wait. I often thought about what it would be like having this dog as a constant companion and having help with the sounds I couldn't hear. You could multiply my hesitation in the beginning by ten and that's how excited I was about getting him. I was thrilled when they contacted me six months earlier than expected to tell me they had a dog for me and a place in the June training class. I had no clue how I was going to manage this dog now that I was without work and would be looking for a new project with a dog by my side. I thought I had at least another two years on the project I had been on, at which point I could bring the service dog into an already existing project. But despite the obvious issues and the naysayers, I went on faith and I planned my trip to California. It is recommended that you take a training partner with you; someone who can learn the process and assist you when you get home because help is sometimes required, especially when it involves teaching him sounds that I can't hear. Due to many circumstances beyond anyone's control, my training partner was unable to attend so I headed across the country on my own. That was not just a step out of my comfort zone but I giant leap!

I arrived in San Francisco at 10pm Saturday night, rented a car and spent the night at a nearby hotel. Check-in in Santa Rosa was not until 4pm Sunday so I awoke the next morning and braved this city I had never been in. I drove to Fisherman's Wharf and did some site seeing on my own. This was a daring and brave move for me but it was the first of many, as I began slowly breaking out of my cocoon. It wasn't as scary as anticipated, proving, as I learned over and over again, that fear is all in the mind.

My three hour drive to Santa Rosa came next. Crossing the Golden Gate Bridge was spectacular, despite a very foggy day and since I arrived in Santa Rosa much quicker than anticipated, I did a little driving around the town, locating the nearby grocery store and a few restaurants. I checked in around 4pm and found my dorm room easily. We had a meeting that evening and classes were to start first thing the next morning for 11 days, with Sunday our only day off and graduation scheduled for the following Friday. That evening, I met the other applicants. There were nine of us. Six females and three males; the biggest class of Hearing Dog candidates they had EVER had! We had varying degrees of deafness but were similar in that everyone had some hearing with the use of assistive devices and we all utilized lip reading as our primary source of communication. Nine total strangers, nine almost instantaneous bonds. Never had I been in one place with eight other people that actually knew and understood what I went through on a daily basis. It was overwhelming. The entire experience was.

So day one they bring out several dogs, more dogs than people, and everyone does a little work with three different dogs while the trainers observe and take notes, keeping in mind, they have at least one dog already in mind for each person before they even arrive. They tell you from the beginning of the process, don't get attached to a dog until we officially tell you it is your final match, which doesn't take place until the end of the week. So I rehearsed this is in my head a thousand times. "Don't pick a favorite. Know whoever they give you is the right one for you." HOWEVER, when they brought out the very first dog for me to work with and said his name was Excel, I was immediately in Love. His name was Excel; it had to be fate because Excel had deep meaning to me. The project I had just completed was full of issues. For more than two of the four years I had to run this entire company from Excel spreadsheets because there was no software on the market able to handle the very unique business model. There were thousands of patients and payments and denials and they were all being handled on hundreds of Excel spreadsheets: payments, billings, denials: EVERYTHING was Excel. There was no way this was a co-incidence. I said in my head "He's mine." Now of course, out loud for the entire day, like everyone else I said, "I don't have a favorite. I'll love any one they give me." But in my mind I was saying "He's mine. I know it." On day two, they assign everyone a dog. It may not be a final match but it is the one they think we will work best with but again they warn, "Don't get attached yet." IMPOSSIBLE – I was attached the very first time I looked into those big brown eyes. So when they brought Excel out of his crate, it was all I could do to stay seated until they said who they were giving him to. And I was sure everyone in that room heard the voice in my head saying, "Mine, mine, Mine, MINE!" AND HE WAS – at least for the moment.

All of those matches made on that second day remained as final matches. I remember looking around that first day and thinking to myself, "Why did they give so and so that dog?" as if I were the expert. But as we gathered around the big table every night to discuss our families, our lives, our challenges and especially our new companions, at one point the confessions began that they didn't understand some of the matches to start either. But by the end of the week it was evident why everyone had the dog they did. Those darn dogs had our personalities! Excel was very serious and business like, just like me. And the others the same. The Diva got the Diva dog with attitude, the over excited, bubbly lady got the over excited bubbly dog. The young college girl that walked with pep in her step got the same in her dog. All nine candidates had dogs that resembled them in some way. It was amazing how perfectly they matched those dogs from information given on the applications about personalities and lifestyles. One of the women joked with the trainers that they did so well she wanted to hire them to pick her a husband!

Every day was a new adventure and every evening we gathered around the big table in the main room: the nine of us and spouses, siblings and parents who were there as assistants, to eat dinner, discuss the day's events and share stories of our lives outside of this safe haven we were calling home for now. For the first three days, the dogs were taken at the end of training and returned to the kennels. Day four, the dogs were coming back to the dorms with us to spend the night. From that point forward, though we were still waiting for confirmation of final matches, they were ours 24/7. We were not allowed to leave campus with them unless on a field trip with instructors but they were ours to feed and walk and groom and care for. Every day from that point after we gathered at the table, we took the dogs for their nightly walks around campus. We stayed up late every night, laughing, sharing and walking with our new companions. Every morning when we came out, sometimes running into each other on our morning walks we immediately started talking about the dogs. Did he sleep? Did you keep him in the kennel? Did he do number two yet? It was like being parents for the first time, comparing notes and giving and getting advice. I don't think I have ever felt that close to eight people in my entire life, let alone in the short time that we got to spend together.

Very quickly the days were passing and with each day a flood of emotions that had us all on an emotional roller coaster. It's hard to describe the emotions as they jumped from excitement to anticipation and even sadness at the thought of leaving each other and this safe haven. But most of all there was the overwhelming gratitude we felt for everyone who gave of their time, talent and love so freely to give us this priceless gift. The volunteers, the workers, the trainers, the breeders and the puppy raisers: The phenomenal puppy raisers. These selfless human beings devote eighteen months of their life to raising these puppies and training them to be the perfectly behaved dogs that they are. Then kiss them good-bye and return them to make someone else's life a better place. It's an indescribable feeling and there is no way to repay the gift that they have given.

All too quickly we were nearing the end of week two. We went from fumbling with trying to hold the leash properly to experts that appeared as naturals handling our companions. On the final day, as the realization of graduation sunk in, so too did the sudden realization that we were leaving this campus ON OUR OWN with these companions in just a few short hours. They were ours and we would be handling them alone without the trainers and without each other. I think for all of us there were mixed emotions. We kept tearing up thinking about going our separate ways and vowing to keep in touch. Then it was preparing for the luncheon when many got to meet their puppy raisers or for me, their breeder caretakers. The breeder caretakers are the ones that have the mother dog, take her through her delivery and name and care for all the puppies for the first six weeks. My puppy raisers were from Ohio and they could not make it to California for the graduation. They did however send me a wonderful letter and a book about Excel and the adventures of his first eighteen months. Again, the emotions were overwhelming and there really isn't a good way to describe it. The puppy raisers and breeder caretakers are seeing the dogs for the first time since returning the dogs to the center – either at six weeks or eighteen months. Either way they had time and love invested into these phenomenal creatures that were now our best friends. The room was flooded with

25

tears of joy and gratitude. One puppy raiser stood up to speak and he said "People ask me all the time how can I do this? How can I raise a puppy for 18 months and then give him/her up?" And he pointed around the room to all of the recipients and he said "This is how I do it. Because I see and feel the gratitude and know that I am helping to make a difference in someone's life." Isn't that what life is about - making a difference for someone else?

Our good-byes were sorrowful but we promised to keep in touch and we have. Several have had the opportunity to see each other again and we keep talking about a reunion for all in the upcoming year. I am so grateful for the friendships I made and for the understanding and comfort of knowing that I am not alone. There are others that understand my challenge because they live it themselves. We are bonded by our uniqueness and that is a gift I am grateful to have had the opportunity to experience.

Bringing Excel, "X" as I often call him, home was a smooth experience, unless you count his fall into the pool and him puking all over my cousin's floor within the first two hours of leaving campus. We made it through the airport with flying colors and he slept the entire five hours home. I kept looking at him saying, "This is it. He's your 24/7 companion." And despite everything, I know with certainty I made the right decision. The months following our return home can be described as anything but stable and routine.

Within three months I relocated twice and after the second relocation I was on the road frequently trying to rebuild my business. I was living out of a suitcase and staying in two or three different locations routinely throughout the week. Despite the fact that Excel had no real opportunity to adapt to any permanent surroundings, he did quite well adjusting and his presence was calming for me in the turmoil of what had become my life. Had it not been for my faith and my X, there were moments I thought I would never be able to go on. Despite the doors that were closed because of the presence of my Angel with a tail, God knew what he was doing and the timing was planned to perfection. I still believe that. And to the doors that were closed, they were not lost opportunities, they simply were not meant for the new road God was guiding me down.

There are many that don't understand the need to have the dog with me at all times. The answer is the need as the outsider sees it doesn't exist 24/7. I assume if I'm in a burning building there will be someone kind enough to tell me the fire alarm is ringing so I can get out with everyone else. However, there is no way for me to know when I may be alone throughout the day. Additionally there are portions of every day that I am alone. And most importantly, fostering the bond and the team that we have become is important. I had someone quite close to me remark "Ever since you got that dog your life revolves around him." Well yes, yes it does. He is a part of me and while I understand that there are some that cannot grasp this it is not for any of us to judge the path of another unless we walk in those shoes. Again, because I "look fine" as people say, they underestimate the challenges.

Overall, most people are accepting of the dog and quite curious. I have had only a little negative response over the dog but those occasions have been rare. They warn you in training that things will happen but you never really believe it until it actually does. But that's ok. Excel has given me so much more confidence and security that when a negative response is voiced, I calmly remind myself it is ignorance of what is not understood that causes inappropriate actions. This is not my issue but that of the other person. I do what I can to help them understand but it is just not for some to understand and that's ok. I have just as much right to participate in all of the opportunities as the next guy and I'm not going to let ignorant remarks stop me. My service dog behaves better than many humans you come across in the course of a day and he was a significant force as I unwrapped the cocoon from around me and emerged as a beautiful butterfly into this big beautiful world of experiences that are mine for the taking!

Chapter II

From the Beginning

The Shape We Take

I was raised in the typical middle class family from suburbia. From as far back as I can remember I was an over achiever who was popular in school. I was an honor student at the top of the class and no matter what I did I had an inherent need to know how to do and be the best at everything. So to the outside world I had it all together: Smart, funny, independent, driven, and apparently normal. Reality had me engaged in a war within so intense that I sometimes got lost in the fray. Daily trying to convince myself that what the outside world saw was me, but inside I was overcome with insecurities, no self worth and constantly feeling that no matter how much I did I was never good enough. It took me years to realize that my outside over achiever was a mask to hide my true feelings of inadequacy.

As children we all fall into a specific roll in the dynamics of our family and the world that we create for ourselves. For me that role was the independent, strong, self-assured one. I was the second of four girls and I experienced middle child syndrome big time. I felt invisible so I attempted from the start to be the best of the best: The best behaved, the best student, the best son my father never had. Outwardly I was driven, while inside I lived my life paralyzed with fear. Fear of not being good enough; of falling short of what everyone expected. Fear of being loved or accepted only on condition. I felt the need to earn love from the beginning and that never changed; it just got deeper. Somewhere along the line it became my way of life: I had to earn the right to be loved, respected and cared for and the way I went about doing this was going above and beyond in everything I did, sacrificing myself and my beliefs and dreams trying to keep everyone else happy. This paralyzing fear severely altered the course of my life. From the earliest days I began to be shaped into someone far different than my original destiny because I feared letting everyone down. Ironically the person I let down the most was myself.

I recall as a child I never smiled much and everyone was always asking why I was sad. It wasn't sadness; it was intensity. I was always so deep in thought, dreaming to devise ways to make my mark in the world. Trying to figure out how I alone could contribute to solving the world's problems. Looking back I often wonder how I, as young as I was, decided to adopt such a huge responsibility. I believe it was divinely implanted, for I hadn't lived long enough or experienced enough to have learned it.

I wanted to be and do so much more but felt inadequate. I felt trapped in a world with too many boundaries. It was like being an eagle stuck in a parakeet's cage. I had these huge wings bursting to take me on my journey but I was confined by this cage that stopped me from spreading my wings. I had a vivid imagination so I lived there much of the time, dreaming of being someone important and making a difference. I was a superhero and a beautiful gospel singer and a missionary saving the world. I was somebody important that the world revered for the good I did. I WAS LOVED! I remember a time when I was about 4 years old when I decided I was going to fly like superman. I convinced myself if you believed, there was nothing you couldn't do. That day I believed I was Superman and I WAS going to fly. There were five stairs from the main floor to the next level with the bedrooms. The main floor had only a living room and large eat in kitchen, side by side. The stairs from the upper level led directly into the long kitchen. I ran down the hall, all of maybe three steps even for a preschooler, and when I hit the top of the stairs I took a flying leap. I spread my arms like an eagle and yelled SUPERMAN! I landed, splat, on the kitchen floor. My mother and my aunt were sitting at the counter that I just landed next to and they followed me with stunned horror in their eyes as I slid the additional three feet along the kitchen floor. I don't even remember my mother asking me if I was hurt, although I'm sure she did. I just remember her chastising me and the words "You CAN'T fly!" echoing in my head. Fortunately, aside from a few bruises, my pride took the worst of the jolt. I was devastated. As crazy as it sounds that was a pivotal moment for me because all I heard was YOU CAN'T! True, it was important to teach me that it probably wasn't a good idea to jump from the top step to try to fly but it was also a missed opportunity for my mother to communicate with me and find a way to encourage me to spread my wings but perhaps not literally to fly. I'm not faulting my mother because I'm quite sure my response would have been the same. Life has taught me many lessons and it is in hind sight I see so many magical moments that turned into indifference due to the inability to see past what appears to be happening at the moment.

Between the age of zero to seven years of age, children undergo rapid growth that is highly influenced by their environment. These are the years the child is forming his belief system and every verbalization a child hears is internalized and contributing to that belief system, either positively or negatively. As I reflected back over my childhood I was able to very quickly pinpoint some significant events in my early years that clearly contributed to my lack of self worth, Superman being one of them, as crazy as it sounds. My parents taught me many valuable lessons about life, family and God. Unfortunately, with no ill intent, many of these teachings had negative connotations and they instilled a fear in me of trying new things or taking risks. They caused me to doubt myself and my abilities. I can't even say I questioned who I was because I never got the opportunity to know. I don't think I am unique in this, for I believe so many in my generation, as children, were consistently being told what we could and couldn't do; how to act and when to speak. Therefore we never got the opportunity to develop our true personalities and discover who we are, or what our purposes in life might be. We weren't taught to express ourselves but to oppress any questions. We were just kids and we were to be seen and not heard. You believed what your parents told you because they were your parents after all and you didn't need any other reason. Our parents were a product of their upbringing, and I mine, and so on. The good news is each successive generation gets smarter. My parents threw away some of the negative things they were **conscious** of, as did I and as my children did also. We joke about some of these things as adults but I realized that the affect they had on me was no laughing matter. We have to learn to break the cycles of negative reinforcement to create self-assured, confident children.

We as parents, even those that consciously work at nurturing self expression and independence, spend a significant amount of time telling our children what they can't do. I remember hearing a comedian joke that parents spend the first year of a child's life encouraging them to grab, crawl, stand, and walk and then the next 17 telling them no, stop, don't, let go. One study estimated that the average child hears the words no or don't 148,000 times growing up, as compared to only a few thousand yes responses. Another study, which is really of no surprise, found that positive interactions and statements by a significant person in one's life relates to high self esteem and that negative interactions are associated with low self esteem. Kids are like sponges absorbing everything around them in those young, impressionable years. I happened to absorb the word CAN'T better than any other word in the English Language. We as adults and especially parents need to make sure that what our children absorb is positive, motivating reinforcement. The kind of inspiration that convinces them they are worthy and capable of doing anything that they dream, except maybe fly from the top of the stairs like superman! We need to be dream weavers. We need to teach them to dream big, and not limit themselves. Fortunately today there are a more significant number of people who believe in the power of positivity. Yet still there are those that find inspiring others is an insurmountable task when they don't find it easy to believe it themselves.

Parents do the best they can with the resources and knowledge they have. Most of the time when we become parents, we talk about what we are going to do different than our parents; changes that are hopefully for the better. I did my best as a parent and I think I did a pretty good job. I know I did the best I could with what I had. I also know there are things my children will say they are going to do different than me. It's the cycle. There needs to be a manual: The **How to Teach Kids the No's in Life - Positively.** We need to learn how to direct them on the why they want to *do* certain things instead of what they shouldn't do. Don't over protect or try to save them from life because it's not possible. Instead, teach them how to do it on their own. I have watched my daughter-in-law with awe in her abilities as a parent. She has taught me so much, as I've watched her begin to shape her daughter into a happy, carefree and confident child. From the time my granddaughter was born she has spoken to her as a person. She explains everything to her which fostered her curiosity and excitement about life. I remember when Camryn was not quite two years old she wanted to climb a tree with me at the park. I took great pride in saying sure, as I sat her on a low branch and hung on to her leg. She looked at me a little puzzled and said 'Grandma I can't climb if you hold my leg.' So I allowed her to climb only as high as my arm could reach hanging on and then quickly diverted her attention to do something else. More recently, while at the park with Camryn and her mother she said she wanted to climb quite a big tree. Now I know she has climbed trees but this one was a little more intimidating so again my protective instinct wanted to hang on to her. Her mother however allowed the child to explore. I sat back and watched, and realized that it was making my daughter-in-law a little anxious also, yet she forced herself to give the child a bit of distance, never taking her eyes off of her. My granddaughter got stuck and I wanted to jump up and run and grab her. But again I watched as her mother calmly walked up to her and gave her instructions on how to get herself out of the situation, instead of saving her. She teaches her, she doesn't save her and she is encouraging her to spread her wings and not be afraid. She is building self-confidence and teaching her to believe in herself and all that God has blessed her to be.

God blesses each of us with gifts that we are to utilize for his glory and for making the world a better place. Sometimes it's hard to distinguish between our gifts and our skills; sometimes they are one in the same. Sometimes we confuse our own needs and desires and call them our gifts. I believe my gifts are that of compassion and service. I can remember as a child experiencing empathy for the pain or needs of others. I had compassion for people that I didn't even know. Whenever I heard of someone or something in need, I literally felt possessed to find an answer. I believed this was my calling but for a young child it was not easy because they were feelings beyond my comprehension and there was no one in my inner circle that could comprehend these feelings any more than me. Perhaps it was because I didn't know how to verbalize what I was feeling, or perhaps it was because those significant adults in my life were not capable of even grasping the understanding of having spiritual gifts themselves.

As a child your inner circle is your family; mostly adult family members. Many of my family are spiritual. My mother was a religious woman who did her best to keep us in Sunday School and teach us about God but in her own limited capacity. She was a 'God Fearing Woman' literally, and she was taught you did what you were told or God would punish you! God given gifts were just not something that normal people got. And she saw me as a child; not realizing that age has nothing to do with what gifts God bestows. For a long time I knew God had a purpose for me but with no one in my closest circle to nurture this it was forgotten, for I had no clue how to understand it; much less follow it.

Behind the Mask

With so many restrictions taking root at such a young age, I began my charade in life long before I even knew the meaning of the word. I accepted my role in the family and my role in life and therefore lived in a whirlwind of confusion between who I was allowed to be and who I was meant to be. The damage to my confidence caused me to build a shell around me to protect my fragile interior, which only further alienated me from those closest to me. Feeling misunderstood, mixed with my feelings of inadequacy and fears of not being good enough, topped off with partial deafness that challenged me daily, I learned to fake it from the beginning. I found my mask. This was my recipe for a life of masquerade. I played a role, like an actor in a play and I did my best to be whatever I thought everyone else wanted or expected of me. I painted a picture of who I thought I should be verses who I really was because, aside from the fact that I didn't know who I was, who I was could not possibly be good enough to gain the acceptance that I needed, it seemed, since the day I was born. When I fell short, the fear of people knowing and not accepting me was devastating, so I hid. Throughout the years I became very good at simply ignoring what I didn't want to deal with. Friends that deceived, boyfriends that cheated; I never ended these relationships, consciously thinking I was loving and accepting people as God wanted me to but knowing now it was because subconsciously I somehow thought that was all I was worthy of. Though my gut told me I deserved better I allowed these relationships to go on.

It was the earliest days of integration and not everyone thought it was an awesome idea. I was in the third grade and I was going to fix this issue. We were all children of the same God and this fuss being made by the grownups made no sense to me so it was up to me to prove them incorrect. One has to ask how someone at the age of eight years old feels so driven to take on such a huge responsibility. But I did and so I went out of my way to be everyone's friend and try to get everyone to be friends. I remember when I was in elementary school there was a boy that used to physically hurt me on a regular basis. This one boy in particular clearly took a liking to me but he was always hurting me. I would go home with bruises because he would punch me. My mother called the school and the kid was constantly in the principal's office getting paddled. My mother would warn me to stay away from him and I would for a time, but as soon as he tried to talk to me or be nice to me again I would try to be his friend, only to return home with some other injury. I remember the principal telling my mother at one point it was my own fault because I continued to be his friend. I didn't know how not to because I truly believed there was good in everyone that just needed to be encouraged to burst out and I wanted to be that encouragement. I was far too young to surmise this at the time but as the years went on and I continually found myself in similar situations, I thought it was unconditional love. I suffered this syndrome throughout my entire life, so that I was walked on and taken advantage of. I was an easy target, even for people that weren't looking for one. But I was not a victim. I was in fact the encourager I wanted to be, I was just not encouraging the right things because there were no boundaries. I had no love or respect for myself and therefore no ability to set the boundaries that needed to be set.

The older I got the more I struggled within and by Junior High, the withdrawal became evident. I shied away from being in big groups or speaking in front of the class. Despite the fact that somewhere inside I longed to be someone special and stand out in the crowd, outwardly I no longer enjoyed being the center of attention and did everything I could to avoid it. I knew a lot of people but I had few close friends. It took me a long time to realize that much of my growing insecurity stemmed from the hearing challenge and the struggle to understand what was going on around me. But there were so many other factors involved that the deafness was almost secondary, especially since we were still unaware of its severity.

The more I matured, the more the issues compounded because there continued to be more variables added to the equation along with a steady decline in my ability to hear; there were more things to fall short of and the risks were higher. I had to be the everything of everything and I somehow learned to navigate around the situations I wanted to stay away from, yet still be a leader. In school I continued to excel and was in all the honors' classes and gifted programs. My peers were running for student council and the debate team while I was spending my time with the under achievers or volunteering at the elementary school. I was safer there and they looked up to me, giving me the importance I needed. Secretly I longed to run for student council but I was terrified of the public exposure that came with it. I graduated in the top 10 of a class of 754 students, was a member of four honor societies and was awarded a full academic scholarship into a local junior/senior college, testing out of most of my required freshman/sophomore classes. Everyone knew who I was; few actually knew me.

All I ever wanted to be from as far back as I can remember was to be a special education teacher and a writer. I wrote from a very early age, mostly poetry and short stories. It was an escape for me and I could express myself so much more in my writing than verbally. But the academic and career advisers informed me that being a teacher and a writer was not good enough for someone as 'intelligent' as me. I needed to be more than a teacher and being a successful freelance writer was not a good career -

that had to be a hobby. So the advisors dragged me to every high level career event that they could trying to help me find where I fit.

One of the events was at the University of Miami, highlighting Women in Engineering. It was a predominately male profession at the time and they were trying to recruit women into the field. The turning point for me at this event was when a very young, pretty woman stood up and gave her story of becoming an engineer and a portion of her speech went something like this:

> *"The best part of my job is I get to go out into the field on the jobsite, with all of these big, well built, sweaty men, put on my hard hat and tell them what to do because I am the boss."*

I said "Ah, I want that job." Why not? I was attempting to find some way to be in control and I wanted yet one more way to display the confidence that didn't really exist. So I began my studies in Engineering. It was against the norm and I always found some way to go against the norm. As I worked to project confidence, I also strived to maintain my feminine side as well. Years ago there was a perfume called Enjoli and the marketing was all about a woman being able to do it all but never let the man forget he was the man. My favorite part of the song was, "I can bring home the bacon, fry it up in a pan, and never ever let you forget you're the man, 'cause I'm a woman." I was going to be the Enjoli woman.

College was torture! I disliked Engineering from the beginning but it was a prestigious choice of career, especially for a female, as it was a male dominated field. I thought it would make me somebody important. My first semester I had a survey class and there was one other female in the class with 18 guys. They split us into survey crews of four and each week we were out in the field surveying. We had all this big equipment to carry so the first day going into the field I remember the other girl in the class picking up the biggest piece of equipment there was. I looked at her, looked at the three guys on my team, picked up the notebook and pencil and said, "Come on guys, let's go." It was my way of taking control but showing I didn't need to prove myself. It worked, the guys loved me and treated me like a lady, even opening the doors for me as they juggled the big equipment and I carried the notebook. I lost that somewhere along the way and years later I was more the one to pick up the biggest piece of equipment, although not in Engineering. I went from the Enjoli lady to Helen Ready's "I am woman - hear me roar!" I'm not sure where the transition took place but hindsight tells me it was inevitable because though I didn't stay in the engineering field, I have spent the better part of my career in a predominately male dominated environment: first in engineering, then executive management and then in operations consulting.

My inherent need to know everything about everything, along with my 'fix it' mentality and my need to be needed gave me the edge in my career and it even helped boost my confidence. I was good at what I did and I knew it. It placed me in positions of authority and I finally felt I had some control in life. I was obsessed with doing it all and being it all. I lived in a man's world where I heard often 'don't be emotional' or 'don't take it personally.' I had to learn to be tough so I spent the majority of my career censoring how I expressed myself because I thought it was necessary to project confidence and gain respect from my male counterparts. I would go down the list: Is that sounding emotional? Am I taking it personally? In many ways I became desensitized. I think I would be referred to as a shark if I were a male in the corporate environment. A less pleasant word is used to describe a female with this characteristic. I didn't like it but my need to be in control took over and it became who I was in my professional life. This too was a constant internal conflict for me because the real me was soft, compassionate and caring well into adulthood and I had a fairly soft demeanor towards others. My predominate personality trait has always been that of peacemaker and people pleaser but as my career advanced this tough guy that I created to protect myself began to overshadow the peacemaker. I never stopped to think before I spoke.

In the modern workforce, there has been a shift towards women owned businesses and there is a lot of talk about speaking from your heart and being authentic. I was born to be the encourager, the inspirer. Instead I was tearing people down on a daily basis. Ironically, the same people I hammered all day I also would scoop up and rescue when they needed rescuing. They must have been as confused as I was with finding the real me. Then, as much as I don't like to admit it, this desensitized personality began to spill over into my personal life as well.

I longed to be loved and accepted and for me the reassurance did not come from those closest to me so I began developing long distance relationships, surrounding myself with acquaintances and distancing myself from any real emotions. The safety in being surrounded by people that aren't invested is that they can't hurt you to the extent that someone close can. I could give and give and get nothing back, or even get stepped on, because I really didn't expect anything more. I somehow skewed my God given gifts and believed I was meant to be a martyr, sacrificing for everybody around me at any cost. I convinced myself by doing this I would eventually impact someone and change a life. What I came to realize, much later of course, was that much of this self-sacrificing behavior was really selfishly motivated, attempting to gain the recognition, acceptance and love that I felt so void of. The void was not somewhere out there; it was inside me. I needed to learn to love myself.

Alone in the Silence

It's odd at times, going through life without much outside noise. I can only imagine what it's like for those that are totally deaf. I had the advantage of hearing much more at one point in life and even now, while I don't hear much, I do hear some. I often wonder though, as I sit outside at night and listen to the silence, what others hear - what does the night sound like? But I adapted. It's human nature to compensate and adapt to our surroundings and our own abilities. I've learned to even tune out what little I do hear sometimes because I have no idea what it is or where it is coming from. This trait was conceived much earlier in life however, as I sunk into a world of silence that had nothing to do with my deafness. It was a different kind of silence that I somehow used as an escape in those early years. I spent hours in solitude as a young teen, feeling separated from the world and its confusion. I was trying to figure out where I belonged and how to hide all at the same time. Control was a big thing for me, even back then, so I spent my time alone because that was the only environment I felt I could control. I could lose myself in my thoughts, dreaming of all the things I wanted to do. Still, despite the lack of self confidence and self worth, somewhere inside I clung to the belief that big things were possible and that someday I would make my mark. It is a wonder, as I think back, how I didn't get sucked into the black hole of depression in those early years. I can only attribute it once again to my faith, for even as a young child I knew there was a power far greater than I and no matter what transpired around me God was in control. I thank God every day that I became an overachiever and not a rebel in those early days because I know it was only by his grace that I triumphed.

Somewhere through the course of this silence my deafness came into play and the world I occupied became quieter. There was a point where the silence I created and the silence I couldn't escape because of the deafness became entwined, although I'm not really sure exactly where the two paths crossed. What I do know is it seems I fought to hear and I fought to be heard most of my life. How silly it seems now, to have been fighting my entire life yet never realizing there was a battle going on. Through the years as I continued to struggle with my self esteem and the degenerating condition of my hearing, the real me simply lingered in the shadows of my life. There were times that I did attempt to emerge but when those times surfaced something or someone would quickly push me back and with each setback I was sucked deeper into the darkness. There is a saying that I have used in business for years that says it's what you don't know you don't know that can hurt you the most. All the searching in the world won't help you find what you're not even aware is missing. I was unaware by this time that I was lost, for I had done so well convincing everyone, including myself, of my ability to do it all. But you can only spread yourself so thin and while I was succeeding on the outside to look like Super Woman at times, on the inside I was exhausted, frustrated and empty. I worked hard to keep up this charade and for me the sad part was I didn't even realize I was in the game. I mean, I suppose at different time throughout my life as the feelings of knowing there had to be more surfaced I saw glimpses that told me this is not who you are but the older I got the more natural the masquerade became. It's true what they say if you tell yourself something long enough you believe it, and then the line between the truth and reality becomes very faded, until they just blend together. My lines blended at some point and I was more convinced than anyone that I was the very image I portrayed for so long. On some levels I was, for it was who I strived to be. The masquerade was to hide the fears and the shortcomings and I was deceiving myself more than anyone.

Chapter III

The Transformational Year

Mind, Body and Soul

O ver the course of my entire life, as each poor decision led to more heartache I was submerged deeper and deeper into the darkness yet visibly life moved on and in many ways, in a positive direction. I can only say that because of my strong faith from such a young age, I always clung to the belief that God was in charge. Even when I buried him along with myself, he was still a deep part of my inner soul and while he allowed me to fumble on my own at times, he never left me alone.

For most of my life I lived a lie, trapped within a shell of existence yet longing to be so much more. Knowing God had a bigger purpose for me but not knowing how to reach it, mostly because I wasn't living as me. I never did. Professionally I was proud of how I was building my career but knew there was so much more for me. Being a single parent most of my life I threw myself into everything for my kids when they were young; I was the room mom, the baseball coach, the Girl Scout leader, the President of the PTA, and the list goes on. You name it I did it. There was no time for myself, which now I know was a form of hiding from myself. My life belonged to my kids and it was exhausting trying to be everything to everybody! So when my son left for college it was a devastating experience for me. I realized that in just a few short years my daughter would be moving on too and then what would I have? Instead of this leading me to decide I needed to build a personal life for myself, it instead led me to throwing myself into my career full throttle. I did great and I advanced into upper management quickly. But just like in my private life, I was sacrificing everything for employers that didn't appreciate it; the more I gave the more they took. I had no life outside of work, mostly because it was safer that way. With my daughter in her teens and not being home much, I spent long hours in the office because I had no reason to go home, nor did I want to. Outside of my kids and my work I had little private life and I liked it that way because I felt protected. I felt worthy because I again convinced myself that the company needed me. I was too lost to even realize it, or maybe care, I'm not even sure which.

My journey out of the darkness did not take place over night. It was over the course of many years of taking two steps forward and then sometimes three steps back. There were many spiritual conflicts through these years, accompanied by those feelings of wanting to be and do more. These feelings were coming back stronger and stronger but life was comfortable on many levels. Comfort is a scary thing because it makes us complacent. We stop growing and we just are. We have to learn to be comfortable with uncomfortable because at least then we know we are moving forward. Money was good and I was finally living without thinking about how I was going to cover expenses. I could get my kids what they needed and wanted which for me was a huge feeling of satisfaction. As a divorced mother, their father was able to be the Disneyland Daddy, giving them all the fun and luxuries of life while I struggled to keep a roof over their heads and food in their stomach. So when the money was flowing I wanted to give them everything I couldn't in the earlier years. I could also help others when they needed it. I offered services for free, gave money freely to those that needed it and continued to stretch myself so thin that there were times I didn't know if I could keep it up. It was at those times I would start to reflect and evaluate my life: You know, those moments when you say, "What am I doing here? What is the purpose? There has to be more."

With each occurrence of self reflection I would take baby steps toward change. I started by deciding I needed to start taking care of me a little more. Always slim through young adulthood, I had put on weight over the years, again part of my cocoon of protection. The weight had become another safety mechanism of convincing myself no one wanted me, instead of risking the pain of being hurt. But as I began a workout program I started to feel better about myself, not due to drastic physical changes because progress was slow. But internally changes started taking place and I began feeling a small sense of accomplishment and self acceptance. It boosted my confidence. The next step was to start changing my eating habits and I moved away from western medicine and began seeking holistic professionals. These were small changes but significant in that it was the beginning of aligning my body, mind and spirit. It was a scary process because it required me to unveil myself in small doses. Sometimes however those doses frightened me to the point of retreat, and I would succumb back into the shadows. But each time I would come back and break through the barrier a little more with every new attempt at freedom.

I began reading everything I could get my hands on: Joel Osteen, Joyce Meyers and Matthew Kelly just to name a few. There were many others because I was hungry and my heart and mind were open to absorbing it all. I read all types of self help, spiritual and business books on being and doing your best. I continued, as I had for many years, to do devotional books, read the Bible and pray. So as my mind, body and spirit continued its course towards alignment, God began bringing more people, better people across my path that made me realize I had few of value around me. And because of my own shield of protection around my emotions I never felt that my family understood me. I knew they loved me but they didn't know anything about me really; or so I thought.

Up until that point there were few, outside of my family that were invested in me. I was surrounded by takers and I allowed them to suck the life out of me. Though fear no longer controlled every aspect of me it still had a firm grip and when I was most compelled to make a drastic move it would take over and send me running for cover. So I was muddling along making minor changes but inconsistency caused the changes to be slow and stall at times. The truth was I still hadn't dug up the root of the issue; I had only exposed bits of it. As the years went on, the moments of self evaluation became closer together and more spiritual. God was really working with me but I was hanging on. Have you ever heard that poem about giving over everything to God to handle and then when he doesn't do what is expected the writer snatches them back from God and says, "Why didn't you handle this?" And God says, "Because my child, you never did let go." That was me. I wanted to do what God wanted me to do but I was trying to control how that would be done. It doesn't work like that as we all know. God will help when you're ready to really let go. With each successful step in the right direction, however slight, I became more and more discontented with life as it was and there was a tugging on me to move my life in a different direction. God has a funny way of pushing us across that line that we move up to but can't seem to get across on our own. When he knows you're ready and it's time, he forces changes upon you so you have no alternative but to leap.

My life and career took a dramatic financial turn downwards and while it was devastating at the time, it was the best thing that could have happened to me. I knew it was God's way of saying, "You were never going to make the move on your own-it's time. I have bigger things in store." It forced me to take a good strong look at myself, my life and face some disturbing truths that I had been hiding from for so long. And it led me back to walking by faith and not by sight, for it is when there is nothing else that we remember to lean not unto our own understanding but on God. It's funny how we turn to God when we are in the midst of struggle and then put him on the back burner when things are going well, or not even going well but we just don't want to disrupt the flow. It is easy to inspire others and talk about faith and believing God is in control when they are facing challenging times. It's an entirely different level of commitment and belief when you are walking through the valley yourself. God took me to the valley so I could reassess not only the mountain tops but also the journey along the way, for it is the journey that holds the deepest lessons and significance. There is a Miley Cyrus song that I fell in love with, The Climb, because it holds such a valuable truth. It's not the speed at which we reach our destination or what's waiting for us when we get there, but it's all about the journey upwards. It's what we experience along the way, how we experience it and what we do with the invaluable information we gather along the way.

Healing from Within

The devastating financial turn that took place was the beginning of the end for me, but in a positive way, for it was to bring an end to my life behind masks. It was the beginning of peeling away years of masks and layers of pain. Here I was, with no income, little savings and a stack of bills for the life to which my daughter and I had become accustomed; a life that now had little meaning as far as I could see. It took some time, but after the initial panic and hurt had passed, I claimed a sense of calm that I never felt before. Calm because I knew God was in charge and it was my time to make some changes. It was a tumultuous year but it was evident to me that the events were falling strategically into place, beginning with the uncanny timing of the call to training to obtain Excel, which divinely fell just after the final week of my last project. It was a risk and many tried to talk me out of it, concerned at how I would find more work with a dog by my side.

So outside of my norm of just doing what I wanted, I prayed, and I listened. And my gut told me to do it, it was the right thing. Often through my life when I made decisions, my gut told me quite the opposite of what I usually did. Sometimes I ignored it because I wanted it and sometimes I ignored it because it was something someone else wanted me to do. But this time I had faith, and I tuned out everyone else and I just prayed and waited for the answer, and the answer was "GO, it's your time." I can't say it was smooth sailing. My mother was ill and needed 24 hour care so my sisters and I were trying to arrange our schedules to do that. Because I was without work we decided it made the most sense for me to move in with her and care for her while looking to secure a new project or find employment, whichever came first. Then my uncle, who was like a second father to me, had a massive stroke. With him in Pennsylvania and my mother in Florida there was no way to be there for each other. So my sisters and I dealt with my mom and my cousins dealt with their dad. It was constant emotional turmoil but I leaned on my faith and believed it was all part of God's big plan.

Upon my return to Florida with my service dog I had two weeks to pack up my house and return to Orlando to care for my mother. I rented my home so at least I had that covered, although I was dealing with tremendous guilt because a very dear friend was staying with me at the time, which meant a move for him as well. I expected to be with mom for six months, maybe more and I was actually looking forward to the opportunity of spending this time with her and bonding. I never felt very close to my mom growing up, for many of the reasons expressed throughout this writing. But later in life our relationship was different; we understood each other better and we had both grown so in our spiritual life.

I looked at this as my chance to confide in her all the changes that were taking place with me and all the crusades of learning and facing who I really was. That was wishful thinking and not what God had in mind, as mom passed exactly 31 days after my arrival. More to deal with and more reason to lean on God for the strength I knew I could not muster on my own. Professionally I sent out over 300 resumes and had gotten little response. The responses I did get were quickly shut down when they became aware of the deafness and/or the dog. It was frustrating but more and more, as I stayed in prayer I began to feel that this too was part of the plan. Mom left a little money that came just at the right time, as everything seemed to that year. A small consulting job also arrived and I used that to resettle back in south Florida, moving in with my son, daughter-in-law and precious granddaughter. I love my son and my daughter-in-law is like my own but it was tough to move in on them. Parents take care of their children, not the other way around. I felt like I was invading their space and in the way. Mind you, this was all me, as they went out of their way to make me feel welcome and I treasured every moment that I was able to spend with my granddaughter. It was a bonding time for us and one that I had felt didn't exist until that time. It's funny how God teaches us our lessons in life. I spent my life taking care of everyone around me, sometimes for the wrong reasons. Now I had to humble myself and not be the savior but the one to be saved.

I've said many times that this was the year I was stripped down to nothing and it was the most challenging time of my life, yet I never felt more alive or free! I never felt so sure of the path that I was on and, in spite of the pain, I was facing my fears and moving in the right direction. Slowly I began to believe in me because I was staying close to God and keeping faith in him. I was practicing what I had preached to so many for so long and it felt good. The future was becoming clearer and while the financial situation was still fuzzy I tried to stay focused on moving in the right direction. I made a decision to take some of the money that my mother left and invest it in me. I did so quietly, thinking my family would think I was crazy. I needed that money to pay bills and this was no time to be spending money for self development. I paid a marketing coach to rebrand my consulting business and incorporated my service dog into the marketing. I began to find more and more ways to step out of my comfort zone and more influential people were crossing my path and leading me to others. I was joining networking groups and creating business alliances. I began taking workshops and investing in myself and my professional development. The more I did, the clearer I thought the path became. I was no longer interested in a long term, secure consulting project. I wanted to start teaching the business owners what they needed to do instead of stepping in and doing it for them. I began to learn how to build more than one revenue stream so all my eggs weren't in one basket. I wanted to reach out and assist those that had a challenge to overcome and show them they were very ABLE to do whatever they wanted to do in life. I wanted to build a successful business so I could begin seriously working on building my non-profit foundation instead of just talking about it. I wanted to start making the difference in the world that I always felt destined to do. And I wanted to write. Not so ironic, when I began to find myself I returned to my original passions: Teaching, writing and helping the challenged. Also not so ironic that my desire to help the challenged would be more meaningful because I was one of those challenged. God's plan.

Aside from the obvious changes taking place around me, I was experiencing much internal change and the emotions that came with that as well. I was discovering things about myself that were painful, which led to many unanswered questions. I remember so clearly the day the light bulb went off for me. The day the truth about me hit me in the face and I suddenly questioned if there was anything authentic or real about me or my life. My friend, my mentor, my lifeline up to the point of my self-discovery, described an actual event that painted such an uncomfortable, but true picture for me that I still cringe when I think about it. It was at that moment that I realized I was so lost that even I didn't know who I was. I was stunned at what I saw. My portrayal of myself to the world appeared to be who I wanted to be, not who I really was. And if that were true, who was this unpleasant person I was seeing now? I had no idea how I would get through it. I began to question everything I believed about myself and who I was.

Have you ever lost sight of your child, or a child in your care, even just for a second? You know that feeling of panic when the thought 'lost' flashes through your mind. At my revelation moment as I like to refer to it, when for the first time I saw a vivid picture of who I had become, I felt that panic. I could not see the good in anything I had done over the course of my life, as it appeared it was all done with selfish and self motivating intentions. For weeks after the fact I experienced anxiety attacks; that feeling of panic in the pit of my stomach and feeling like I couldn't catch my breath. It was like I was a stranger to myself and I feared I would never be able to regain my footing. People I loved continued slipping away and it seemed my life was unraveling before my eyes and there was nothing I could do to stop it. I tried not to question the Divine plan that had turned my life into what seemed to be an endless tailspin, but I have to admit at times it was exacting. It reached a point where the material depletion was not significant and I was able to leave the mystery of how I would pay my obligations in God's hands. But when people dearest to me continued to slip away there was such a deep sense of loss that there was a point I thought I would not be able to go on.

So few people ever penetrated my safety shield and while even these people didn't fully know me, they were the few that I trusted with pieces of my heart. The very people that helped me to face myself and my fears and really see who I was gave up on me; left me when I needed them most. Maybe they were never really fully there, but I felt so abandoned. I was still trying to keep the brave face that I did for so many years for my family but inside the pain was unbearable. I cried, I prayed and I journaled, trying to figure out who I was and what happened along the way. I never felt more alone than I did in those weeks, because I felt like there was no one to talk it out with; no one who understood. I had to do the only thing left: Lean completely on God and my faith. I prayed and each day I said, "God, this is your day and I thank you for giving it to me. I thank you for all that I have and all that you are preparing me for." And I continued to put one foot in front of the other to keep moving forward. Baby steps. Sometimes that is all we have and that is all we can do!

As I struggled to make sense of the stranger revealed to me, it finally occurred to me that loving unconditionally had to start within yourself and for yourself. How could I possibly love others if I didn't even love myself or see myself as worthy? I had been living as a chameleon for years because I saw no value in me. I began to realize that I allowed time and space to come between me and my true friends to avoid being dependent on anyone because it was not easy to continually let go of people who came in and out of your life when you really cared about them. I never revealed all of myself to anyone from the fear that they would see me as not good enough. Fear that they would see me as I saw me for all those years. Sadly the very thing I feared became reality, but not because I wasn't good enough; it was because I wasn't honest about who I was. Unfortunately for me it was inevitable because I had played the charade for so long that I forgot the reality somewhere along the way.

More and more I was ready to accept that I wasn't superwoman. I didn't want to be her and I ached for meaningful relationships with people that I could count on, not just them counting on me. I was always a Giver but I had to become capable of being a Receiver too. For it was in learning to receive that I discovered my deepest ability to give with true intent. I had finally realized my giving bank had long been drained and it desperately needed replenished. I didn't want to be the "I am woman hear me roar" character but I had become incapable of exposing any vulnerability and I thought asking for help was a sign of weakness. Even if someone wanted to give me the opportunity to lean on them it was my own inability to accept it that prevented me from having the very thing my heart ached for most. I had to become vulnerable to break the shield around me. As devastating as the revelation was, it was the turning point for me to rediscover me, the true person that I had buried so many years before. So as I embarked on the journey of this rediscovery, I realized that many of my gifts became skewed and they became driven by my inner need to be accepted and loved and be SOMEBODY! Slowly I was able to take off my blinders and look at my life head on, overcoming the fear of what I would see. The calm after the storm made me realize that though there were times I was driven by my own pain and need to be recognized there still existed the desire to do for others, the ability to feel the pain of others and the unending passion to make the world a better place. The only thing that really changed was the need for recognition which was replaced by a longing for the chance to accomplish big things in a quiet way and give all the glory to God!

After half a lifetime I was finally emerging from my cocoon and recognizing the beautiful butterfly inside. I realized that the statements and incidences I let define me as a child were incorrect and that it was time to let go of the paralyzing fear that I allowed to hold me back. I began spreading my wings again and it felt good. Life began to change and my priorities were being rearranged. My gratitude was growing despite the undesirable place that my life appeared to be in because there was a deep peace that I never felt before. I began to believe that every day truly was a gift and even in the darkest hours there are Blessings lying just beneath the surface. We have to take the time to look and continually show our gratitude for all God gives us.

It took me awhile to realize if you want people to believe in you, you have to believe in yourself. People will become Takers unintentionally simply because it is made easy for them. Setting boundaries doesn't mean you don't love the other person; it simply means you love yourself as well and unconditional love has to start within. It became easier to embrace my differences and not feel like they had to hold me back. I prayed constantly, asking for guidance in every decision I made. I became aware of the quality of the people that were crossing my path and looked for the purpose. I could see things happening that I knew were events strategically planned by God and even though I wasn't sure where they were all going, I embraced them and thanked him for what he was doing. Still financially the situation was not turning around. It seemed with every positive result I saw there was a counter. My consulting business was not picking up. Was I networking enough, was I making enough contacts, was I doing enough? I kept asking in my prayers, "Show me. What am I doing wrong? Why is this not turning around?" I was exhausted, frustrated and confused. I cried and cried and prayed, looking for answers that didn't seem to be coming.

And then, early one morning after yet another sleepless night and many tears I was drained. So I lay quietly, eyes closed, focusing on God and repeating what I had so many times before, "Be still, and know that I am God." After several minutes my eyes just shot open and it was literally like a light had been turned on. I sat up and said out loud, "Stop focusing

on making money and focus on making a difference."
I knew exactly what that meant. I had been talking for
more than three years about building a non-profit
foundation. My vision was so clear I could actually
see the interior of the facilities and had the perfect
people selected for certain positions. I dreamed
about it, I just kept putting it on the back burner until
I could gain my financial stability. Well this was it -
forget the stability. It was time to follow my heart; to
stop looking at the money and follow the dream in my
heart. It was placed there for a reason and it was time
to get my priorities in order and let God take care of
the rest!

Healing takes time. You don't get over in a day
what took a lifetime to create. I lost people along
this journey. Some moved on to a higher place,
some moved on to follow their own dream and
some well, just moved on. But sometimes we just
have to let go even when we don't want to; even
when we can't see the sense of it. Life doesn't
always make sense. It is not always suppose to.
Sometimes God reveals what he wants us to see and
sometimes we have to walk by faith when we can't
see where the path is leading, knowing that He is
leading us in the right direction. Holding on to
something or someone who isn't really invested
anyway holds us back and causes us not to make the
moves necessary to move forward and be who we

were meant to be. It's better to face the pain, let go and let God handle it so He can move you forward.

We all have a purpose, a divine purpose that, if nurtured from the start will blossom earlier in life. For those of us who let go of the gifts and the passion long ago, it's not too late. We will be late bloomers but we can still bloom. The day you are able to take off the mask, look yourself square in the eye and say I AM WORTHY, is the day you can start the change. This will be the day you can start dreaming big once again.

Meet the Authentic Me

I spent my life believing I was giving 100% to everyone. I was trying to be the best I could be but at the same time trying to feel good enough. The calm after the initial storm made me realize that I couldn't possibly be giving 100% because I didn't even have 100%. My giving bank was dry because I had not thought to resupply it. Even superheroes can lessen their powers if they don't refuel. We cannot possibly give continuously and take care of everyone else if we never stop to take care of ourselves and our own needs. Boundaries are necessary and the person responsible for setting those boundaries was me.

It was time for me to be accountable. The more I evaluated myself, my life and the choices I made the more I realized I wasn't the monster I thought I was at that moment of revelation. What I found on that day was a human, with flaws and shortcomings, but also with brilliance and passion and meaning. There was a scared little girl trapped inside that believed she was unlovable because she had flaws; that she wasn't good enough because she couldn't please all of the people all of the time. She convinced herself that the self sacrificing antics made her worthy of God's love. I freed that frightened little girl and it was then that I discovered ME, with all of my flaws and shortcomings, but infinitely worthy. It was at that unleashing that I reclaimed the real me; worthy of having feelings and desires and needs. Worthy of knowing I was a child of God and He loved me with no expectation. I did not have to prove myself to Him which made me realize I certainly didn't have to prove myself to anyone else. I discovered that the true person inside had all of the intent of the one that I portrayed; she just sometimes fell short because she was human.

I am an honest, trustworthy person who will do whatever is in my power to protect the ones I love and the ones who deserve protection. I am a person of integrity whose true passion is to make a difference in the world and believes that if I can touch one person and make a difference in just one then it is worth it. I am a person who loves giving and doing for others, but no longer at the cost of losing myself. I do believe that most people want to be and do good and sometimes they just need someone to believe in them. I also believe that I am worth protecting. I believe that in life you should give first because it is in giving that we receive. There is also a difference between putting others first and not even putting yourself on the chart. I learned too that I don't have to be a tough guy all the time. The fact is that I never was; I just pretended to be. I can be vulnerable and I can expose my fears, my desires and my dreams and not be afraid of what others think. They are good enough because they are mine and it is my journey that I'm living, not someone else's. If I stay in tune with God and pray about everything first he will guide me. I will make it to my destiny because He is leading the way. I now realize I don't have to do it alone. I don't have to control it all. So come and meet the authentic K-LO.

My "Be Thyself" Manifesto:

BE THYSELF

> *Keep God first in everything I do and know that he is making the crooked path straight for me.*
> *Be true to myself and who I am.*
> *Never let anyone sway me from my true beliefs.*
> *Have faith that everything turns out as it should.*
> *Always have an attitude of gratitude.*

Forgive my past and know it has helped shape who I am today.
Live for today.
Laugh often.
Remember a smile is free.
Dedicate myself to be of service to others first.
Stand for something with meaning.
Be Honest.
Be Authentic.
Always be proud to speak the truth.
Listen to my inner voice.
There is no such thing as failure; each step is a stepping stone to success.
Always go forward with confidence.
Remember that I am worthy.
Be kind.
Be compassionate.
Be empathetic.
Enjoy life.

Life doesn't happen to us, it happens *for* us. If we open our heart and know that God can make good even out of what appears to be unfortunate, then we know that all that happens in our life serves a purpose. I might consider my past life a waste because I wasn't living with true intention but I don't. It wasn't. It was a significant part of my journey and I did a lot of good over those years. I helped a lot of people and I impacted lives, probably more than I will even know. And most importantly who I was and my experience in life shaped who I have become. It doesn't matter how long it takes to discover your purpose. Learn who you really are, accept who you really are and be who you really are PROUDLY! Don't let one more day go by allowing anything to stand in the way of being your Divinely Awesome self!

I have begun to create a circle of people that support and inspire me. Some have always been here and some are new but they all inspire me and encourage me to keep moving forward. I am saddened for those that moved on and I still question, for some, why that had to be, but no matter how sad that makes me, it cannot take away the joy of finding me again: Of knowing who I am, what I am and that I have a purpose that I am following. I still don't know what the future holds, but I know one thing for certain- God is in charge and he is guiding my way.

Between Two Worlds

Chapter IV

Just Saying

They say necessity is the mother of invention. Well this holds true when you are confronted with situations that you must learn to maneuver through: Thus, the art of lip reading. I learned to lip read without even realizing it. I simply found myself staring at peoples' mouths instead of in their eyes when they spoke from as far back as I can remember. I've always wanted to take a formal lip reading class to see if it would boost my ability. Some people seem impossible to read and I've often wondered if there were formal tricks of the trade that would help with those people. You have, for instance, those people who barely move their mouths when they speak, or those who move it in such a distorted fashion that you wonder if they have some muscular control disorder because whatever they are saying is not comprehensible. Then you have those that seem to be in a race to get the words out before they forget the thought.

As good as I am, these are sometimes impossible situations. A friend once said that I was so good at reading lips that I could read his lips in the car behind me through my rear view mirror. That was a bit of an exaggeration, but, if I do say so myself, I'm as good reading through the rearview mirror as I am face to face. Again it was necessity. When my kids were small they were always trying to talk to me from the backseat. Most people use that mirror in the car to check the cars behind them. Mine was aimed at one side or the other of the car so I could talk to my kids when they were in the back. Hey, I had side mirrors for the cars. You do what you have to do to get through the tasks at hand.

I always felt the need to be totally prepared for every situation. I am the person that arrives early to big events and when planning, everything is ready and I'm sitting waiting for the arrival of the guests. When traveling, you'll never find me running for a flight. I'm at the gate an hour early, strategically placed and staring at the desk so I won't miss the attendant's call for boarding. Now when they begin calling, they always call in sections and I never know when it's my turn so as soon as they start boarding I begin to move toward the gate. More than once I got the nasty attendant that would look at my boarding pass and chastise me saying "It's not your turn yet" and actually make me move to the side. So then I began to wait until the very end to get in line so as not to be reprimanded. As I look back now, free to be me, it was absolutely crazy the insignificant situations that I allowed to cause me stress. So a few years back, still not through my metamorphosis but taking baby steps towards change, I decided to tell the attendant as soon as I arrived at the gate that I would need assistance. Now, what I should have said was I am deaf and I would like to pre-board because that's what I really wanted. Baby steps. Instead, I went to the desk and explained that I was deaf and would not be able to hear when my section was called for boarding, thinking he would suggest that I pre-board. If you don't say what you want you can't expect anyone to know. So after explaining my dilemma to the nice young gentleman, he leaned over the counter, took my boarding pass into his hand, holding it where I could see it, and while pointing to the area where it said the section, he V E R Y   S L O W L Y said, "Y o u a r e   i n   s e c t i o n   C,   s o   w h e n   I   c a l l   s e c t i o n   C   t h a t' s   w h e n   y o u   b o a r d." Now I stood their staring at this young man a bit perplexed, fighting the urge to let my Pittsburgh sarcasm take control. Instead, I gave him my biggest dazzling smile and I nodded and said, "Yes sir, I understand, and thank you for that explanation. The issue will be that when you say section C is boarding", then I gave a bit of a pause, pursed my lips, squinched my nose and shook my head in a no fashion, "I won't hear that." A bit embarrassed he said, "Right, you said that didn't you?" Well yes, yes I did. So then he said, "Stand right over there and I'll signal you when it's your turn." So I did as he told me and as expected, he forgot me. So I waited until pretty much everyone was in line and my Pittsburgh sarcasm could no longer be contained. I walked over to him and kind of waved to get his attention. Then with a bit of a smirk on my face I said, "I take it you called my section already, yes?" NOW, when I travel I go to the gate and say, "I am deaf and I wish to pre-board please." I'm concerned about them labeling me as disabled but clearly my challenge is miniscule as compared to most walking around who consider themselves 'normal.' Just saying.........

They say laughter is the best medicine and I believe it to be true. I mean, in all of life's craziness, sometimes you just have to laugh or it can drive you over the edge. I've learned to appreciate the idiosyncrasies of some people and understand that it is only through lack of understanding, and sometimes even genuine desire to make one feel less awkward, that they behave in such a crazy, irrational manner. At times, it's not so funny but I've learned not to take it personally and remind myself when the responses are less than polite that the issue is theirs, not mine.

I've compiled some of my favorite experiences here, either personally, or as relayed to me by other deaf individuals, hoping it will educate some and if nothing else, share a few good laughs.

I Read Lips, Not Tonsils

This is one of my favorites: Why, when people discover you are a lip reader do they suddenly open their mouth wider than the whale when it swallowed Jonah and then they suddenly start to talk like they are in slow motion replay? I think I can speak for all of us lip readers out there when I say we are really not interested in viewing your last meal as it lies in the pit of your stomach preparing for digestion. It's even more perplexing when this takes place after they've been holding a conversation with you for several minutes, all the while talking normally. They turn their head once, raising the need to say, "I'm sorry, I did not catch that, I read lips", and it's downhill from there. They suddenly find the need to shout and over enunciate at a speed slower than Pluto making its orbit around the sun. I mean really, can anyone read that slow?   And what's with the shouting? I'm deaf – that's not going to help. Sometimes it's all I can do not to burst out laughing in their face but at the risk of making them feel uncomfortable, I bite my lip and stifle the laugh. So a word to the wise: lip readers read lips when you speak clearly, not too fast and enunciate normally. Shouting, over enunciating and slow motion is only going to initiate stifled laughter, not understanding. Just saying.........

I'm Sorry, but Your Head is Not Transparent

I love when I tell someone "I'm sorry, I need to see your face because I can't hear, I read lips" and they say okay, then look the opposite direction and keep talking. Is this a trick? Do they want to see if I'll answer? Sometimes I have the greatest urge to say "Well I'm deaf but you're apparently slow." Seriously, what am I supposed to do with that? There have been moments of frustration, or maybe just defiance, that I blurt out something like, "I'm not sure if you know this or not but your head is not transparent." Or I just let them ramble until they finally need a response and realize I am not responding. When they turn around I say "Oh, were you talking? I didn't know – I have to see your lips." So if someone says they read lips make the assumption they are telling the truth and look at them when you speak. But please don't refer back to number one and start over enunciating. Just saying.........

No I Will Not Lip Drop (Eavesdrop) For You

If you want to be the belle of the ball, just let a few people learn that you are a lip reader at the party. This is more a situation that happens when you are a teenager or young adult (I HOPE so anyway). People who have never taken the time to even say hello to you suddenly are very interested in getting to know you. Momentarily that is so they can ask you what Joe across the room is talking about. I am not a spy and it takes such concentrated effort to speak to the person next to me I have no desire to try to figure out what someone across the room is saying; at least not intentionally. Ok, I've picked up a few remarks at a distance but quite unintentionally I assure you. You know, those people that because you can't hear they think it ok to stand across the way, then talk about you very low because you can't hear them. Again, they never take you seriously when you say you read lips so it never occurs to them that they are looking your way as they speak. I've had a good laugh myself on occasion when I've repeated what a person has said about me or another, thinking no one would ever know. But still, I don't intentionally ease drop on conversations and it doesn't matter how much money you offer me, I'm not going to spy for you so don't waste your breath. Just saying.........

The Service Dog Dilemma

It's really very comical the things people come up with when you have a service dog. They see the dog, then take a quick scan of you from head to toe, like they're checking you out. Nope, can't identify anything wrong with this one. So now curiosity has the best of them (don't they know what curiosity did to the cat?). Is the dog in training? Is he a comfort dog? Or how about "Do you need to hold my arm?" Ahhhhh, NO. I can see fine. But even after being informed that no assistance is needed to walk, they offer you warnings "Watch out for the pole." I can SEE the pole so unless it's going to try and tell me something I don't think it's an issue. I think the best one I've heard so far is the dear old lady that was in the post office when a friend entered with her service dog. She was one of the few people to actually read the bright orange logo on the vest that said "HEARING DOG." So she very seriously contemplated the sign for a few minutes and then asked my friend if the dog was deaf. Now this dear old soul was totally serious so my friend had to fight the urge and stifle the laugh while she explained the dog was fine, she was the one that was deaf. And they call us disabled? Just saying.........

From the Mouths of Babes

The innocence of a child is one of the refreshing things in life that never changes. There is no sensor device from the brain to the mouth so they say what they think pretty much as it comes to mind. Some adults use this technique as well but it's not quite as refreshing after you are out of single digit age. But the kids, you can always count on them to put a smile on your face just with the sheer innocence of their remarks. So what does a child say when their parent tries to explain that you are deaf, which means your ears don't work like they should? Things like "Did you get a little bit electrocuted?" or "How did you break your ears?" My all time favorite was "Did your mama whack your head between her hands when you were a kid because you weren't listening?" (I think this child's parents may need closer examination). Just saying………

Yes, I Do Look Fine

This one is a biggie and is said often. When you tell someone you are deaf and you read lips, a common response is "But you look fine." As opposed to? What does a deaf person look like exactly? Sometimes I think that if people would slow down just for a second or two and allow their brains to catch up with their mouths they wouldn't make such ridiculous remarks! I look fine. I feel fine. I am actually fine, thank you very much. Just saying.........

No Laughter Here

So at times the remarks and the ignorance is no laughing matter. At times it's insulting and demoralizing so don't assume because we politely say nothing that it's ok; it's not.

The biggest one for me personally is when someone is trying to tell you something that you don't understand and you say 'excuse me' once, twice and then the third time when you still can't understand they say, "Never mind it wasn't important." Let me just say that is infuriating! If it wasn't important why did you say it in the first place? You may as well say, "It's too much work to try to make you get it and I don't want to take the time so never mind, I'll go talk to someone else." If I am going to put the effort in trying to understand what you have to say to show you that I believe what you have to say is important, then you should show me the same courtesy by taking the time to help me understand. Often, if you reword your sentence it helps because there is sometimes only one word or two that is creating the lack of understanding.

Another biggie is when I am in a restaurant or conversation with a group and I don't understand what someone is saying to me. Often I will look to whoever is with me hoping they will know how to reword the question/sentence for me to understand. Unfortunately, rather than rewording it for me they, trying to be helpful, jump in and respond for me. This is a definite NO NO! What normally transpires after this is the person will now address whoever answered for me instead of me. If you find yourself in this situation, to assist the deaf person repeat what was said for them but let them respond, they will feel much more appreciative instead of a nuisance. Just saying.........

Chapter V

Life is for the Taking

Not Dis-abled, Differently Abled

For many years after becoming cognizant of my deafness, I pretended it didn't exist. I never considered myself to have a disability despite the deafness. There were two reasons for this. The first was that no one ever treated it like a disability. Many people in my father's family inherited varying degrees of deafness but it just was. There was no preparation for successive generations; you either got it or you didn't. The second reason was for me personally, I don't like the word disabled; it implies that I cannot do something and if there's one thing that will make me do something, it's telling me I can't. I liken it to when you tell a child no. Whatever was just labeled as off limits, they now want with every fiber of their being. I never grew out of that.

There was no conscious embarrassment that I felt about being challenged. It was just awkward and for the most part I was able to get along and no one really noticed. Well, no one but me that is. I was carrying a burden far heavier than needed because not sharing this challenge openly caused me to compensate in ways that secluded me from the world even more than what I had already done. When it was necessary for me to share or someone noticed I had hearing aids I was fine discussing it. I just didn't like to be the one to bring it up. Again, this had way more to do with my own devaluing of myself than with my inability to hear. So at one point I did become known as the girl with the hearing aids. Labeled. Your entire life people label. You're somebody's child, somebody's sibling, somebody's spouse, somebody's parent. Everyone goes through some or all of these label phases I'm sure. I was even labeling myself and then buying into it. For me it became the girl with the hearing aids and more recently it became the lady with the service dog. Crazy as it is, even these seemingly harmless labels contribute to a sense of loss of identity when you're someone struggling to know who you are. When do I just get to be me? I'll tell you when. For me it was when I stood my ground and realized that these labels did not define who I was nor what I was capable of. I had to develop my voice for people to know who and what I was. That voice has to echo loud and clear because if you never say who you are how can you expect anyone to know?

There is a stigma that goes along with being challenged. People will avoid a person with special needs because they are not sure how to handle them or how to react. For me it became the lack of ease that accompanied trying to communicate with me. It was just easier to avoid me. So then I began to avoid people, both out of fear of not being able to understand them as well as the discomfort when it became evident they were avoiding me. I spent a great deal of energy convincing others as well as myself that I was not disabled and my challenge was not slowing me down but I was slowing me down to avoid the discomfort of the reality and I did this the better part of my life. For too long I lived in my world of solace internally, while externally I paraded as a self confident woman and leader. It was quite ironic as I look back, for I was the wind beneath many sets of wings and the igniter of smoldering timbers for others, yet I was incapable of believing in myself. My own disbelief was masked because I projected self assurance, trying to buy acceptance and find just one person that would say "I believe in you."

When I began my metamorphosis out of that cocoon, emerging from beneath the pain and insecurity, I realized it had been a steady game throughout my entire life; the pieces were just sometimes different. I had a tough exterior, portraying I could handle anything while the frightened little girl cringed on the inside attempting to avoid any situation that may cause a stumble and less than stellar performance for the watchful eyes of the world. We cause our own insecurities by magnifying a minute spec in the sand into a giant boulder. As I was emerging from these layers I lived beneath for so long, and let me tell you it was a scary process, I realized how utterly ridiculous my fears were because they were perceived notions of the unknown. Fear is an innate emotion that can paralyze, so when fear arrives we have two options; we either **allow it** to stop us from moving forward, or we face it head on. If we simply ask ourselves if there is any real danger attached to what we are imagining in our minds, we could then rationalize that the fear is imagined. Danger is real; fear is imagined. So if you are standing face to face with a lion then yes it is likely that real danger exists in that circumstance and I would guess there will be some emotion such as fear attached to the situation.

In most situations, the only power in fear is the power that we ourselves give it. Decide today that your word is FAITH not fear and clear all thoughts of anything except the greatness God placed in you. We are here to enjoy the exquisite journey of life that we are destined for. I was astonished to discover that I had allowed myself to become very disabled but it had nothing to do with my hearing. It had to do with the paralyzing fear I imagined and then allowed to take control of every aspect of me. I had to learn that the only thing limiting my development and my ability to be the best me that God intended me to be was **ME**! Freedom comes when you stop and face that very thing that you have spent far too much time and energy hiding from. If you are not willing to take risks in life you will never reach your true potential; that's how the best got to be the best. It is the ability to breathe and be comfortable in your own skin, knowing that your best **is** good enough and you are uniquely made to be uniquely you. Don't hide from it, embrace it! For me it was liberating and for the first time I was actually feeling as alive as I had tried to simulate for all those years!

So now as I've rediscovered me and all that I can be, I freely admit and embrace that yes I am partially deaf and the degree of my deafness continues to decline. How far it will decline only God can answer but I can't spend one more minute thinking about it. It does exist and it makes some things more interesting for me. I am abled differently but I am well able to do anything that I set my mind to! We are all challenged in one way or another. It is not the challenge that defines us but rather how we handle it. For me, I choose the Be-Abled mentality. Nothing is impossible, for I'm Possible! Don't be afraid to do and be all that you can be. When God is leading you down a path that appears uncertain to you, follow. For the places he takes you are far more spectacular than any you can find on your own.

Look Out World, Here I Come

I never realized the depth of friendships that I was missing because I felt like no one understood, but experiencing these friendships has made it easier for me to expose myself a little more to others as well. What I came to realize is everyone needs to be understood and when you're not you become somewhat of a recluse, retreating inside yourself those areas of your life that you think no one quite understands. I was still out there in the world, living and making my mark; impacting people without even realizing it. My calling has always been to make a difference in the world but because I was insecure I was searching for some big bang that I thought I needed to make. I thought I had to be successful by the world's definition, with power and control, for people to hear me. I was searching for some way to say what I had to say when all the while I was saying it, without ever uttering a word. I just needed to believe in myself to see it.

As I was building my business I struggled with the marketing aspect; with this whole idea of knowing who your 'niche' market is and learning how to speak directly to them. My 'niche' market was every business according to me. I could never quite define it any smaller than that. This was much the same in every area of my life. I felt like I had to be big and bold so people would listen but it was the quiet subtleness of the example I set as I marched through life that made the biggest difference. I remember my father once told me "Whatever you do you always have to do it over the top." We laughed about that through my whole life. I wanted to be noticed. The reality was I wanted to make a difference but I misconstrued that into being larger than life. I came off as arrogant.

One of the biggest lessons in my life was when I hired my sister in a business I was running as a consultant. My intent was to give her an opportunity to grow and build a career. She was so smart and funny and had so much to offer but because of choices made early in life she never went to school so she struggled with landing a well paid position. I was going to give her that opportunity because I knew she could handle it. So I hired her and tried to push things on her and make her learn and do more and build a career. I was going to 'save her.' The laugh was on me. She didn't need to be saved. While she appreciated the opportunity and the pay was better than she had made in the past, she was not open to the stress and pressure I was putting on her. The day she told me I was 'arrogant and condescending' was the biggest slap in the face and it stung but it was a reality check.

I built a career and became a work-a-holic, giving more and more because I thought it made me more important. I made good money and I was able to give things to people because of it. I loved being able to do that and I loved the feeling. But it was when I lost it all that I realized much of what I did was to validate myself and be accepted by others. In a sense, I was trying to buy my way into some sort of status position to be worthy of being loved. Who the heck did I think I was that I was big enough to save the world? Maybe they didn't need or want saved. My sister certainly didn't. Yes, we can make a difference in the world but we can't save anyone; that's God's job. I am merely a messenger and no bigger than anyone else here. My biggest differences were made quietly, when I thought I was seemingly unnoticed. Those are the moments that count the most; the moment when you are "The One" for someone else without even trying. The moment you talk to a stranger in a restaurant, when you volunteer to help someone in need; not because someone sees you but because someone needs you. These are the moments that truly count. Oh there are definitely times we need to stand up and shout but we need to do it with joy and honor, not arrogance and bravado.

What I learned was to use the obstacles of life as building blocks; all of the obstacles, especially the ones that are easiest to hide behind. Build upon them to make you better and stronger and more resilient. Every one of us has challenges; some invisible, some clearly visible. But whatever the challenge, don't use it as an excuse to stop you; use it to propel you forward. Use it to be an inspiration for the next person trying to figure out how to get past it. Find the advantages you have because I guarantee if you really look at your situation, you'll find you have an advantage in some way. Over the years many times people would say to me, "You're amazing, no one would ever know you have a challenge." I would say what's the big deal? For me and many like me we never saw the awe in our ability because we learned to adapt out of necessity. However, now when people express amazement in what I can do and have accomplished and say "How do you do it" I no longer say "What's the big deal." My answer now is this: "First I did it because I had to and now I do it because I know I can." We are all amazing with amazing and unique abilities. No one can do or be exactly as you can so stop, reflect and give yourself credit for your own awesomeness. We are all divinely awesome in our own unique ways! Do I still hesitate? Yes, sometimes I find myself preparing to put on the mask or my cloak of concealment. But I catch myself much more quickly. I stop myself faster and it makes it that much easier the next time. I've come to learn and accept that the disability is not mine; it is constructed by exclusion and prejudice that is placed upon me, which makes it someone else's issue.

As I continue on this journey we call life I have learned to accept where God has me in each moment of time gratefully. I thank him for even the not so awesome times. As I said before, things don't happen to us they happen *for* us so we need to keep our hearts open for the lessons and the direction He is guiding us. We should start each day with gratitude for who and where we are, knowing that we are EXACTLY how and where God wants us right now in this very moment in time! I began this journey feeling stuck between two worlds; one of silence and one of sound. What I discovered is in reality there is **only one world** and it belongs to all of us. How we choose to live is exactly that: A Choice. We can choose to dwell on the negative or choose to be happy and make the best of what lies before us. Every day is made up of choices and we are responsible for making them. I choose to turn my silence into the wonderful sounds of life, music, laughter and love! The fact that I cannot hear these things with my ears is not relevant; I hear them with my heart and that my friend is the sweetest music there is! Live life everyday with the intention of being of service to others for if we are all working together for the good of all that is when we will begin to really make a difference. And WE CAN MAKE A DIFFERENCE!

Chapter VI

Meet the Divinely Unique

In the course of my journey over the past year, I have met some extraordinary people with extraordinary stories of determination. Some were barely acquaintances, some were just passing through and some have become life-long friends, but all have impacted my life and served a definite purpose in my own journey of rediscovery. Following a few share just a small part of their individual story, showing just how successful and Divinely Unique we all are!

Meet Jacquelyn Gioertz

Jacquelyn Gioertz has spent many years living in Europe and traveling the world. Her life has been spent teaching others to understand the magic in their lives

and to follow their passions. She is an avid student of the Universal Laws and an Energy Healer.

As a Transformational Thought Consultant, Infinite Possibilities Trainer, Author, Speaker and Artist, her goal is to inspire and empower women to embrace their uniqueness and find their strengths to create the life they love and deserve.

Treasure Your Flaws

Remember when your mother warned you about playing with sticks and other pointed objects? She probably said, "It's all fun and games until someone loses an eye!" It's true. When that happens, it becomes a life lesson. I know this because at the age of 3or 4 I had the good fortune to be hit in the eye with a stick, causing almost total blindness in my left eye. Now, I'm sure my family felt that it was a tragic accident and a terrible thing to happen to such a small child. My brother, who was at the other end of the stick, probably didn't see the good fortune in it either, but that's another story.

At the time, all I remember are the many visits to the eye doctor. These visits were invariably associated with eye drops followed by the ever present eye patch. I'm not exactly sure how long this healing process took, but I do remember being told, "As soon as the blood behind the eye is absorbed, vision will be restored." As it turns out, the doctors were not right. The only portion of the vision that was restored was a small portion of my peripheral sight, of which I am extremely thankful.

Having been faced with this condition at such an early age, it was easy to adapt to the differences in vision and I began to compensate automatically. With only one eye you live in a 2 dimensional world. There is no depth perception and it's very difficult to judge distances between objects. Sometimes it's not easy to tell if the distance is a few inches or several feet. It didn't pose too much of a problem once I got the hang of it but to this day I still sometimes miss the glass when pouring a drink, or reach to put something on a table and let go a little too early, missing the table and having the object hit the floor with a crash! And I will never enjoy those cool 3D movies that have become so popular because for me they are just a blur, with or without the special glasses.

Even with these adjustments, the only real downside I can remember was that, because of the blow to the eye, my left eye was not straight and it always looked to the left no matter where I was actually looking. Totally not cool if you're a kid in school. It was very distracting and the source of much ridicule. We all know children can be very cruel and it was not unusual for my mother to find me in tears upon returning home after a day with my fellow students. Fortunately at the age of 9, my mother found an organization that would cover the costs of surgery to have my eye straightened. The surgery was scheduled and soon my blind eye was able to follow my good eye. Vision wasn't restored, but at least for appearances, it looked normal again.

I tell you this story, not for pity or sympathy, but because I learned so many things that I otherwise never would have learned.

I learned that I am not a victim. I am not different than anybody else. Being so little when it happened - I don't remember what it was like to see with both eyes, so I learned to do things I wanted to do, even if it took a little extra effort or practice. And believe me, it certainly did take extra practice! I did acrobatics, routines on uneven parallel bars and baton twirling. I even competed in baton twirling and won medals!

These were things that normally require depth perception and no one expected that I would be able to do them. I did them anyway and I mastered them! At times frustration would get the better of me, but I persevered and just did it. My most frustrating and at the same time proudest accomplishment, was learning to play squash. Now, for those of you who aren't familiar with the game, it's played in Europe and is pretty much like racquetball except the racket has a longer handle and the ball is smaller and faster. It requires speed on your feet and in your thinking and yes, it requires depth perception. I was determined to learn the game and play it well. I practiced resolutely and I remember so clearly the hours of watching that ball go sailing past me about 12 inches from the end of the racket. It took me a while, but the brain is the most amazing tool we have. The more determined I was, the more I thought about it; the more I practiced the better I got. What you think about, you bring about. You create your reality with your thoughts and actions. Before long, my brain allowed me to automatically compensate and know where that ball would be and how I had to hold my racket in order to hit it. I not only learned to play but I learned to play well and actually won a number of tournaments.

My message is two-fold: First, NEVER let anyone tell you that you are NOT capable of something. Only YOU can decide just how capable you are. Second, learn to have and show compassion for other people. Don't judge so quickly, as you watch someone challenged with parking their car, or making a really wide turn, or some other seemingly annoying behavior. I say be patient and understand that person might not have the same faculties that you do. We often assume everyone has a perfectly functioning body to work with, but that's not always the case.

Because of my own challenge and experience as a child, I taught my own children to NEVER, EVER make fun of someone or something that appears different than the norm. I taught them to be conscious of what they say and do so as not to cause another to feel hurt or inferior.

Although these messages may seem medial, they are profound insights that help make this world just a little kinder; a little gentler. As I walk my life path and am confronted with people being irritated and grouchy, I often smile and give them a gentle reminder that other people are not intentionally out to aggravate them (well, not usually) they are just doing the best they can with the resources they have. And that's alright.

I leave you with this thought. What are your 'flaws'? If you look closely, I'm sure you will discover your own treasures in them and recognize that they have contributed to you becoming the amazing person that only you can be. No one else on this earth has exactly your abilities, and no one else on this earth can use your abilities. Be YOU and enrich the world with the gift of YOU!

Meet Megan Kennedy
and her mom, Sonia Moscatelli

Megan & Mom

Megan Kennedy was the older of Sonia Moscatelli's 2 children. Moving into her final semester at University of Nevada in Reno, Megan will graduate with a Bachelors in Psychology in December 2013.

Her goal is to attend law school and become a Civil Rights attorney, specializing in the rights of the challenged and working closely with the Americans with Disability Act. Sonia has worked as a special education teacher her entire life, never knowing that she herself would be faced with the challenge of raising her own child with special needs. She shares her story of raising her extraordinary daughter.

Standing on my Own

Megan & Ras II

The greatest thing about not being able to hear is the silence. Silence to hearing people and silence to hard of hearing/Deaf people are two very different things. Hearing people have the creaks in the house, the sighs of the wind, the dust of traffic and the rhythm of breathing in their silence. My silence, as hard of hearing, is like a blanket straight from the dryer in December; all encompassing, relieving and heavy. It is fabulous to sink into this silence at the end of a day filled with noisy people, crowds and stores. It is frustrating to push against this silence when you're trying to hear on a cell phone in the middle of Walmart on a Friday evening.

Living between the worlds of hearing and not hearing has become a place to stand on my own two feet, but it was not always like that. I was born with a genetic condition called branchial-oto-renal syndrome. I had no outer ears and my middle ear structures were abnormal, with bones fused together to prevent any sort of total recovery. There was little known about the condition so doctors reconstructed my left ear in the hopes that it would restore some of my hearing. Unfortunately, it had no real impact and I will have moderate to severe hearing loss in both ears forever. Because I could not wear the traditional over the ear hearing aid, I wore a bone conduction aid on a spring-loaded headband until I was 17 and was a candidate for the BAHA implant (bone anchored hearing aid).

Reflecting on my childhood reminds me how fortunate I was, and am. I went to school, played with my friends and lived comfortably. My parents kept their 'grown up' realities between the two of them and I grew up wonderfully naïve. At the age of 17 I made the decision to move to Reno, Nevada and attend the University of Nevada, Reno after graduating high school and receiving a scholarship. I had assumed that college was going to be an amazing experience, filled with friends and boys and parties and would turn me into a successful, poised human being who would land a great job. My basis for this reality was grounded in the movies, and reality certainly did not fulfill any of my expectations.

The first 2 ½ years of college were difficult for me. I was an expert in avoidance. I had been able to effectively forget about my hearing loss for most of my life. I didn't need to talk about it, because it didn't affect my life. I didn't need any special services because I could do it myself. I was stubborn to a fault. In college, however, classroom acoustics meant I would fail if I didn't accept a little bit of help. I received a program called TypeWell, where a transcriber accompanied me to my classes and transcribed the lectures onto a laptop for me to read. As much as I disliked this, I needed it. Around this time, I also submitted an application at my mother's urging to Canine Companions for Independence (CCI) for a hearing dog. I figured nothing would ever really come of it, because I didn't really need it.

By the time the call for Team Training came a couple of years later, I was drowning in a black hole of self-deprecation and loathing. I was stuck inside my head and my bed, focusing all my energy on school and spending most of my free time sleeping. There was no point in trying to do anything, because I couldn't seem to do anything right. CCI required its prospective handlers to attend Team Training, a two-week stay at their headquarters in Santa Rosa, California in order to learn how to handle the dog and I begrudgingly accepted. Up until the night before I was due to leave I doubted my decision to accept the spot. Why was I doing this? I wasn't in a wheelchair. Why was I selfishly taking this dog away from someone who could actually use it? Questions popped in my head like fireworks and I almost didn't go. The doubt was torment.

I went anyway, figuring that if I got there and it was not good, I could always leave—CCI gave us that option, and I reminded myself of it as I stepped into their dormitory on their beautiful grounds. I settled into a room that was equipped with a hospital bed and a fully wheelchair-accessible floor plan. The doors had flashers on them, so when someone knocked they would light up and tell me that someone was at the door. I had never seen something like this in my life. The dogs that would be circulating through our group were placed in the room on the first day of Team Training, and we were allowed to approach them. They were all so beautiful; yellow and black Labradors peering back at us with curious faces. The very first dog that I approached was named "Ras II", and she was the smallest of the bunch with a tiny, perfect little face. I was totally smitten with this dog—something clicked between us at that moment, but I pushed it away. We didn't get to pick our dogs, and as the instructors began to make matches, I didn't even get to work with Ras. I watched jealously as my classmates got to handle her. I thought I had felt something with her, but I admonished myself not to be disappointed.

To my complete surprise, when the instructors announced matches the next day, I had been paired with Ras. We embarked on the most amazing two weeks of my life together. I met a group of people that I will always remember. I shared things with them that I had never talked about with anyone else; they understood frustrations and fears that nobody else could. We were all scared and insecure at times, even if they did have 20 plus years on me. Confronting myself and learning from it was the most healing experience to date. I gained a lifelong partner in Ras. After a year together, I have come to rely on her for things I never thought that I would: my alarm clock in the mornings, a door knock, smoke alarm, microwave timer. I can live in my own apartment because of the freedom she grants me. What Ras ultimately gave me, however, was so much more than companionship and a peace of mind.

The best thing she gave me was strength: the strength to face myself, to accept myself for who I was and have the strength to speak up about it. She didn't push me to it, try to give me advice or tell me that I needed to do anything. It was a quiet sense of comfort that crept up and it was life changing. I know that my life is only just beginning and that I will continue to learn, change, and grow. But my perspective has shifted and my desire to help others has intensified. After my graduation from UNR in December of 2013, I want to apply to law school and become a civil rights attorney, specializing in the rights of individuals with disabilities and work with the Americans with Disabilities Act. I know there is no way of knowing if that plan will work out, but life is exciting again. I have goals and dreams and the fear is no longer blinding. It is just strong enough to push me forward into hope, with Ras by my side.

My mother has been next to me the whole time and without her, I never would have applied or gone to Team Training. Her own perspective, while different from mine, has become an important part of our relationship and will remain an indelible connection between us forever.

Sonia Moscatelli shares with us her perspective and the challenging decisions of a parent raising a child with special needs.

A Mother's Love

Raising children is one of the most challenging jobs there is. And then you have a child with a disability and there are so many more challenges. As a first time mother everything is over-whelming and joyful at the same time. When Megan was born I remember being so elated, scared and filled with a bit of uncertainty. Due to Megan's lack of outer ear structures I did not know if she had hearing or if so, to what extent she could hear. An Auditory Brainstem Response (ABR) Test was completed when she was one month old and it was determined she had a moderate to severe hearing loss. This was the best news I could have received!

With the news that Megan had some hearing I immediately consulted with an audiologist to have her fitted with a hearing aid and to determine our next steps. Fitting Megan with a hearing aid, however, proved a bit challenging. Since she was unable to wear a behind the ear hearing aid, we consulted with a hearing aid company to have her bone conduction hearing aid fitted onto a headband which she would wear around her head. I will never forget the shocked expression on Megan's tiny face the first day I put her hearing aid on and she realized that the television actually had sound! Beginning at three and a half months of age Megan wore her hearing aid continuously and never once complained about having to wear it.

Throughout her life Megan had a fabulous team of doctors, audiologists, and speech-language pathologists. Their knowledge, expertise, and advice along our journey truly were a gift. As a first time mother I relied on their knowledge to steer me and help me make the best decisions I could make. The decision to send Megan to a general education public school was one I didn't take lightly. I visited a Hard of Hearing class and a general education class and knew that hearing peers would provide Megan with good language models and opportunities to develop and use her language. While at school Megan had access to a language rich environment and at home I worked on her ability to lip read and to 'practice' using her hearing when people didn't look at her or when there was other noise present. Hours of speech therapy and practice at home helped Megan develop sounds and pronunciations of words she couldn't hear. Hours of having me stand behind a door and having her repeat words enhanced her ability to 'hear' in the hearing world. As I always told her, "People don't always look at you when they speak to you." I'm sure all those tireless hours of work were not much fun to her, but I do feel they better prepared her for the real world and the challenges it presents.

Supporting Megan throughout her years of growing up proved to be a wonderfully fulfilling experience. As a young child she was curious and wanted to learn about the world around her. Her love of learning transferred to school where she excelled in her studies and earned many top scholastic honors. However, in addition to her scholastic achievements her empathy, compassion, and perceptive insight into others continue to amaze me. She has and continues to develop into a well rounded insightful person.

I would like to take the credit for all of her accomplishments and things she has done so far, however, that would be unfair. Megan deserves all the credit. She has worked countless hours and her determination and courage to persevere through anything is remarkable. Even though the world can sometimes be a judgmental place she has shown us through grace, resilience and a great deal of work that dreams and goals can be achieved. She is an extremely bright, talented and driven young lady. Her ability to overcome her challenges and obstacles still awes me to this day. She has taught me so much and I am so proud to be her mother.

Meet Ancil Tyrell and his son Trent

Trent Tyrell is a 24 year old young man who lives with his father Ancil. Ancil has dedicated his life to Trent, refusing to place him in a home for persons with special needs. A Business Analyst by profession, Ancil made the bold decision in 2002 to leave corporate America and pursue a career where his passion lies, in Health, wellness and fitness. This is the story of a father's love and determination, told by a third party.

Impossible is Not an Option

In 2009, Ancil became a single dad to his then 20 year old son, Ancil Trent, or Trent as he is known. Trent is special. He was diagnosed as 'educatably retarded' shortly after his birth on March 23, 1989. Ancil's life forever changed at that moment, but even he didn't realize the extent of it.

Trent cannot read or write. He cannot tie his shoes. He cannot care for himself. He can dress himself but inevitably something is on backwards and his shoes are on the opposite feet. He can communicate but not always clearly. He has no real concept of time. Everything is now or tomorrow. He repeats constantly which can pretty much drive anyone to drinking after so long. Ancil doesn't drink. That's a good thing.

When children are born, parents spend the better part of their life teaching them to spread their wings and fly. They anticipate with excitement their high school and college graduations, the career path they choose and the mate they choose. They dream of what it will be like on their wedding day and when that first grandchild arrives. Not Ancil. Not for Trent anyway. Ancil will never experience Empty Nest Syndrome due to his son growing up and moving on. Trent won't. He will experience all of these things with his other children but it won't replace the pain he feels for his first born son. Even so, Trent brings a different set of learning experiences and Blessings.

Trent is special. He has special needs but he's also very special. He lights up a room with his smile. He can drive Ancil to the brink of sanity but he loves unconditionally. Trent loves the ladies and the ladies love him. He inherited his father's charm. He is smart in so many ways but it's like it's locked inside and he has no way to get it out. He is often restless and frustrated at times. He's bored. His life consists of going to school, watching TV and eating. He loves to eat. Trent cannot hold a pencil to write his name but he handles his fork like a samurai warrior handles his sword. His biggest pleasures are Starbucks coffee and dancing. He does a great booty dance! He loves to travel too. He always wants to go on Jetblue or to the Bahamas. In reality, you just have to take him to the local hotel and let him have room service and watch movies; movies he doesn't sit through because he has no attention span.

Ancil doesn't complain. Trent is a challenging responsibility but a Blessing as well. Ancil knows this and he counts his Blessings. Ancil comes across as a saint to those on the outside, with the way he handles Trent and the patience he has. But Ancil berates himself at times for not having more patience; for reaching his limit. He doesn't give himself enough credit. God only gives special people to special people. Trent struck it rich with Ancil. Few single fathers would take on this responsibility. Ancil wouldn't have it any other way, but life is complicated.

Ancil is a fitness instructor. He is a business analyst by profession but left corporate America to pursue his true passion; to serve others in the areas of health and wellness by aligning the body, mind and spirit. He has a huge place in his heart for kids. He grew up in the YMCA in greater New York, after emigrating from Trinidad and Tobago. He stayed strongly involved in the organization because he realized there was no substitute for spending quality time with youths. He has a goal to develop high functioning programs that help adolescents transition into successful adults, both professionally and personally. This includes his fitness programs for kids, which will utilize volunteer teens to work with the younger children. The first of these programs has already been started in a local charter school. It also includes fitness programs for special needs persons and an annual Father/Daughter dance to foster that ever important relationship in a young girl's life. His passion is huge and his determination to make a difference seems to be what carries him.

It's not easy, when his livelihood requires him to travel throughout the day and there is no reliable means for Trent. His daily schedule is controlled by Trent and hinders his growth. He is not in a financial position to hire private care for Trent, which is expensive. State money that is supposedly available is not easy to obtain. Very little is known about getting it, even by the professionals in the field. People have been on state waiting lists for funding assistance for five, eight, or sometimes ten years and have never received anything. Once someone is receiving, there is no system in place to re-evaluate to determine if they still need the funding or if it can be better used elsewhere. Few ever actually get off the waiting list. Trent gets his social security only; nothing else.

Special needs persons can attend the public school system in special education classes until they turn 23, at which time they are out of the system. Programs are few and far between for these special needs adults. Private facilities are very expensive. State programs are short on funds and usually there is a waiting list or concern for leaving your loved one at these places. Some say Trent is lucky because he was called from the waiting list at a local adult program. Ancil doesn't call it luck. He calls it divine intervention. School starts at 9am and ends at 1:30pm. There is an afterschool program but Trent no longer participates in it because of the scheduling conflict. So Ancil has to be at the designated drop-off for Trent daily. Transportation is another issue. County funded transportation is available in Broward County but leaves much to be desired. It's unreliable.

Often runs very late. No way of knowing when it will actually show. Trent has been left alone on the sidewalk before. Once he was on the van for over three hours. The school is only 30 minutes away. After school Trent often spends his days on the road with Ancil. Summer is another story. There are more kids than slots for summer camps. Often Trent spends his summers at home, which means he's on the road with his dad most of the time.

Every day is a challenge for Ancil. Constant scheduling. His schedule, Trent's schedule, the School schedule, the Transportation schedule. Did I mention that Ancil has two other children that are very important part of his life as well? They live with their mother. More schedules, events and visitation. Life never stops for Ancil. Days start at 5am and don't end outside the house until 8:30-9pm. Because he's on the road most of the day he doesn't eat well. He teaches others about the importance of proper nutrition and sleep but doesn't have the luxury of fitting it into his own schedule (Don't do as I do, do as I say.) He's on the road most of the time, traveling from one client to another, to the gym, to meet Trent's van, etc. Some days Trent stays with him all day, traveling from client to client. Some days he gets dropped off with his brother for a few hours. Either way, it means Trent too is on the go from 5:00am until 8:30-9:00pm on most days. Ancil worries about Trent but Trent doesn't seem to mind. Once home, Ancil has to feed and shower Trent, then get him to bed. Finally, he eats himself, normally not before 11pm. Exhausted, he has two to three hours more work ahead: paperwork for clients, scheduling, billing, workouts. On an early night he's in bed by 1:00am but more often than not it's closer to 2:00am.

How long can a person, even one in good physical shape like Ancil, keep up this grueling schedule? He goes on three or less hours of sleep most nights and little food to fuel him. How long can it last? If you ask him, as long as it takes. He won't give up his passion and he won't give up his son. He's an inspiration. He has the drive, he has the knowledge and he has the ability. Most would say all he needs is one good break. Ancil would say 'Divine Intervention'. So he waits, patiently, with faith, for God to open the right door; the door that will turn everything around for him to fulfill his dream. The one that God chooses!

Meet Denise Perez

Married to Louie in 1991, Denise is a woman that fought her way through life from the beginning, yet managed to stay positive and know that God was in charge and leading her along the way. This story is only a small part of a much larger story of determination, perseverance and faith! There is always so much more than meets the eye!

Breaking Free

After receiving my health vaccines at the age of two, I developed Rubella with a very high fever. The fever burned the nerve endings in my ears causing total deafness. They gave me this assistive device that was considered a hearing aid but it was big, bulky and I had to wear it around my neck. I couldn't stand it so I kept throwing it away until my parents finally gave in and I didn't have to wear it any longer.

After consulting with doctors, specialists and speech therapists, the decision was made to mainstream me, offering no special schooling or the use of sign language. As per the doctor's recommendation, due to my young age, I would easily be able to adapt and build my independence. It was true it did build my independence, though I don't believe I would define it by using the word 'easily' as he did. I spent years with speech therapist to develop my communication skills. I have a not so fond memory of my first Speech Therapist: He was a tough man and after slapping me across the face for not pronouncing a word properly, my parents moved me, looking for someone with a bit more compassion and a little less tough love.

Growing up was rough. Kids can be unkind and unfortunately so can adults when they lack the understanding and patience to deal with a challenged child. I went to private school through the fifth grade and in those days the private schools were tough on you. I often got lost in class because teachers wouldn't make the effort to make sure they were facing me. One even said it wasn't her job to give me special attention; she had a class to take care of. Another sent me to the principal because she couldn't understand what I was saying. I even got paddled and I'm still not sure why but that was it for the private school.

The following year my parents placed me in public school, hoping there would be more compassion. I was fortunate that I had a wonderful teacher! She was supportive and nurturing and for the first time I felt like somewhat of a normal kid, for she treated me like everyone else and that was all I really wanted.

The older I got the more I perfected my speech and the doctor was right, the more independent I became. I'm not sure I totally agree with the concept used to get me to that point because along the way I became tough in an effort to protect myself. I felt like I had to fight my way through life and somehow it didn't seem fair. Still, the end result was I became fiercely independent, not looking for excuses but solutions.

By the time I reached high school I had developed a sense of security within and was determined to show the world I could do anything. Though still in the public school system, I was attending a new school that was opening for the first time. Because they had split the districts, I would be attending school with an entirely new group of kids so no one was aware that I was deaf. I liked that I wanted to keep it that way, at least until I began making friends. I decided to try out for cheerleading in the weeks before school began without revealing my secret because I wanted to prove I was just as capable as everyone else. They had roughly 400-500 girls try out and there were only 12 slots but I was confident because I knew I aced the try out! On the first day of school one of the others told me they were announcing the squad over the PA and they were going to be announced in the order of scores, with the highest score being announced last. I panicked. How would I know if my name was called or where in the scoring I fell? How would I know to react or not? As I sat in my English class contemplating how to handle this and still keep my secret, I noticed the boy sitting right in front of me. I don't know why but he seemed to be a nice guy and I decided to trust him with my secret so I scribbled a note explaining my dilemma, my name and asked him to let me know if was called. I also asked him to please not reveal to anyone else that I was deaf. The poor guy agreed but was sweating heavily; I guess concerned he might have to tell me I didn't make it. Plus he had no idea they were calling in the order of scores so the more names they called that weren't mine the more nervous he got thinking I wasn't going to be called. When they finally called my name, this guy jumped out of his seat and said U DID IT, U DID IT!!! I not only made the squad but I had the highest score. He was both astounded and intrigued that I had accomplished this being deaf. We became close friends and remained so through the years. Word began to trickle out that I was deaf but still the majority of students and staff were unaware. About three months into the year I was called into the office to be interviewed by a young man. I didn't know him but assumed he was doing some sort of paper for a school project or perhaps the school newspaper because he was asking me questions about my hearing impairment and cheerleading. Much to my surprise I learned he was a reporter for the Miami Herald and about a week later an article came up with a picture of me and the headline, "You Don't have to Hear to Scream." The article released my secret to many now at the school and when I returned to school the next day everyone was over enunciating and/or shouting at me. These were the same people that had been talking to me since the start of school normally but now that they knew I was deaf they felt the need to change that. I did the only thing I could think of and talked the same way back to them. Insulted a few, made some laugh but I think they got the message; I'm the same person I was yesterday, talk the same way you did then.

I excelled in high school and was involved in many extracurricular activities. I joined the drama class and on talent night I was in a group with two other girls and we were to perform an improvisational skit. We practiced somewhat what we would say and how we would do it. When it came our turn to take the stage I got nervous. The curtain opened and the lights were blaring on us so it made it impossible to see the audience. Panic set in and my mind went blank, leaving me standing there staring out into the blackness that was the audience. I started to whisper under my breath (or so I thought) an explicit, "Oh, sh%$, oh sh%$" over and over. I glanced an my partners who were staring at me with horrified looks on their face and I just assumed it was because I was not speaking. Since this was improv, I wondered why they didn't jump in to save me by taking over but they stood there pale and dazed. After what seemed to be an eternity, the stage lights were dimmed and the audience lights were turned on. People were roaring with laughter, including the drama teacher. I was at a total loss, as I could not see how everyone thought this was so funny. The drama teacher finally composed herself, made her way up to the stage and pointed upward, explaining to me that the microphones were on and the audience could hear everything I was saying. The only thing I could say was, "Oh sh$%!", which started another round of laughter. It was in fact Improv and the drama teacher gave us all three A's, stating it was the funniest and most entertaining skit she had ever witnessed. Who knew how easy it was!

Upon graduating from high school I received a scholarship to MDCC and got my AA degree before moving on to the University of South Florida to continue my education. While there I was receiving no assistance so I worked two jobs while going to school full time. Due to unforeseen circumstances I was unable to complete my degree at that time and I never returned.

Instead, I began a 25 year career working in the Insurance industry and becoming quite an expert in the Medical Insurance arena. Unfortunately, despite my knowledge and proven track record, I was passed over for promotions time and again. One could only surmise this was due to my deafness because people tend to avoid what they don't understand.

It was faith and determination that got me through life. Then God blessed me with a wonderful man who loves and supports me unconditionally. Outside of God I always felt that he was my saving grace and sent by God especially for me. He always told me if I wasn't happy in my career I should leave, perhaps retire early. This was a struggle for me because of my fierce independence. Up to that point, though I thrived and accomplished many things, proving to everyone my challenge would not hold me back, internally I felt that I had spent my life fighting to prove myself. I was tired and frustrated. I decided to seek counseling to help me resolve the internal conflict that was taking place. God led me to a wonderful counselor that helped me to realize I didn't have to fight or prove myself to anyone. I could look at my life and all that I had accomplished and be proud, not bitter. So I took my husband's advice and I retired early. We have a wonderful life!

When you live between two different worlds, it can be lonely at times, feeling like no one understands. I now wear a Digital hearing aid which has been amazing for me to hear so many things I never heard before. It took some time and patience getting used to but I love it. I can honestly say that I survived my challenge by the grace of God and his Angels. The road was not always easy but I believe now it was worth it. Until recently I never believed there was anyone that understood my journey. Then I met Karen and realized I was not alone and now I feel that there is a new journey just beginning! Where it takes me I haven't a clue. But this time I know I'm not alone!

About the Author

As a senior leader with 20 years of experience partnering with existing and start-up companies to establish processes and documentation, budgeting and staffing requirements, in 2007 K-LO Enterprises, Inc was formed and Karen, a/k/a K-LO, began working as a Business Transformational Consultant. She is an expert in business operations and through her years of experience, has identified the key areas where gaps arise, enabling her to quickly diagnose the weak links and recommend an action plan to improve the health and vitality of a company. In addition to consulting services, she also offers a series of workshops to address these key gap areas for both new as well as established businesses. She is characterized as an ambitious problem solver who utilizes an analytical/quantitative approach to break down organizational barriers, identify and structure process driven business transformations.

Born with a degenerative hearing impairment, Karen has been overcoming obstacles since before she even knew they existed. Though 75-80% of her communication is done through lip reading she has never labeled herself as disabled and has learned to embrace her uniqueness. Despite the challenges she has never let them stop her from moving forward. "I never say I can't because I can't hear. I CAN, I just sometimes need to do it differently than others."

Embracing her uniqueness also involved realizing that accepting additional help at times was not a sign of weakness but a sign of strength. Therefore when the deafness became a safety risk, she pursued the avenue of being partnered with a Hearing Dog. After almost two years on the waiting list with Canine Companions for Independence (CCI), she was partnered with her service dog in June of 2012.

"As a Consultant I do a lot of work with Excel spreadsheets. I had just completed a project where I actually ran the entire company off of spreadsheets for almost two years, while designing custom software. So you can imagine my surprise when they brought me a dog and said, "Meet Excel". I knew from the moment I looked into those big brown eyes he was soon to be an Angel in my life. He has become my best friend and guardian, alerting me to those sounds I cannot hear on my own."

With a strong passion to be of service to others, K-LO is now utilizing her expertise in business operations as well as her personal story to encourage and assist others faced with challenges to embrace their uniqueness and be all that they can be through her *Differently Abled* Community. ***Between Two Worlds: Bridging the Gap from Silence to Sound,*** is her first book which tells of learning to embrace your uniqueness, remove the masks of fear and self doubt and rediscover your true identity and all that you were meant to be. She is active in the non-profit community and is currently working to establish her own non-profit, with plans to open the first of *Heaven's Houses* in early 2014.

For more information about Karen Londos, visit her website at www.k-loenterprises.com. For speaking engagements email her at k-lo@k-loenterprises.com